The
OVERWHELMED
BRAIN

Personal
Growth
for
Critical
Thinkers

Paul Colaianni

Ulysses Press

Published in the United States by:
Ulysses Press
P.O. Box 3440
Berkeley, CA 94703
www.ulyssespress.com

ISBN13: 978-1-61243-639-5
Library of Congress Control Number: 2016950676

Printed in Canada by Marquis Book Printing
10 9 8 7 6 5 4 3 2 1

Acquisitions editor: Casie Vogel
Managing editor: Claire Chun
Editor: Renee Rutledge
Proofreader: Shayna Keyles
Indexer: Sayre Van Young
Front cover design: what!design @ whatweb.com
Cover artwork: © elwynn/shutterstock.com
Layout: Jake Flaherty

Distributed by Publishers Group West

IMPORTANT NOTE TO READERS: This book has been written and published strictly for informational and educational purposes only. It is not intended to serve as medical advice or to be any form of medical treatment. You should always consult your physician before altering or changing any aspect of your medical treatment, including the guidelines as described in this book. Do not stop or change any prescription medications without the guidance and advice of your physician. Any use of the information in this book is made on the reader's good judgment after consulting with his or her physician and is the reader's sole responsibility. This book is not intended to diagnose or treat any medical condition and is not a substitute for a physician.

Contents

Introduction

My childhood and early adulthood up until the age of 20 was shaped and molded by a dysfunctional upbringing. Now, at 46, after a lot of healing and education, I've gone from sabotaging every job and relationship I've ever been in to a place where I feel at peace most of the time.

But the path to peace was not easy. It has taken years to uncover, process, and release buried emotions and deep-rooted sadness and anger.

The trauma I experienced in the past pales in comparison to some of the stories I've heard from my clients and listeners of my show. It wasn't until I started *The Overwhelmed Brain* podcast and blog that I learned just how much abuse and neglect exists in the world, at all levels.

I never really thought that I had it worse than anyone else because I had no idea what a "normal" childhood was supposed to be. After learning about the struggles of so many other people, however, I realized just how easy *my* childhood was.

And that's a very sad statement to make, because children that have gone through *any* level of trauma may have no reference to what could be worse, so their experience is always going to be the worst thing that ever happened to them.

Since *you* are the only one that experiences your life, *only you know your suffering best.*

I wrote this book to serve as a gateway out of that suffering so that you can get to an empowered place inside yourself.

When you are empowered, you'll make decisions that are right for you. This means that instead of making decisions based on the fear of consequences, you'll take steps that honor you at your core, moving you toward a mentally healthier version of yourself.

The hardest part about getting to empowerment is evolving beyond the beliefs and perceptions of childhood thinking. Your past has shaped how you view reality, and you've taken what you learned as a child into the adult world, thinking that the same rules apply now as they once did.

The truth is your *entire world* changes once you become an adult. When you leave home, get your own place, and start living life on your terms, you experience a world you've never seen before. And if you're still carrying around many of the beliefs and perceptions you had when you were a child, you may not be equipped to handle what comes your way.

This is especially true if you were brought up with any type of abuse, trauma, or neglect.

The coping mechanisms you learned in childhood may not serve you as an adult. When you were a child, you figured out how to respond to the world around you so that you could *survive*. That seems like a strong word because you may or may not have been in an actual life-threatening situation. But when you were younger, you didn't know if that was true or not! And the more dysfunction you experienced in your family growing up, the more likely you created beliefs about people and the world that aren't necessarily true anymore.

Holding on to beliefs that you created during a dysfunctional childhood helps to keep you dysfunctional, at least until you adopt a new belief system or are able to heal from some of your past hurts and traumas.

Of course, it's possible to have a great childhood and still develop beliefs that don't serve you as an adult. After all, trauma comes in many forms with different levels of intensity.

The best way to tell if you have beliefs that serve you or not is to look at the results you get when going after what you want most in life. If you want a fantastic relationship but keep attracting hurtful or abusive people, you probably have beliefs that keep drawing you to the wrong people.

If you lose job after job, you probably have beliefs that cause you to behave a certain way to get you fired. Or you get to a certain point in your career then quit because you're burnt out or you've lost your passion about the work.

Life throws challenges at you left and right. When you're prepared, you'll have the resources you need to survive almost anything that comes your way. By the time you're done reading this book, *you will have those resources.*

You'll also have a better understanding of why you do the things you do and what you can do to create more peace and less stress in your life.

Much of what stops us from getting the life we want is wrapped up in beliefs that aren't working, values that we aren't even aware of, and perceptions that cause us to see reality in a way that isn't resourceful.

By the end of this book, you'll be able to clearly identify the beliefs that don't serve you, you'll be in alignment with values that drive you, and you'll have the courage to embrace the full expression of yourself and live life from an authentic place.

There is a path to overcoming your overwhelmed brain. Are you ready to take the first step?

CHAPTER 1
How Do You Show Up in the World?

Do you consider yourself a victim of circumstances, or do you see your life as the culmination of your own decisions and behaviors over the years?

Best-selling author Alan Cohen once said, "You are in integrity when the life you are living on the outside matches who you are on the inside." Integrity is a great word because it represents full, honest expression of self. I also call this *congruence*. When your thoughts and intentions match your behavior, that is congruence. But if you say or think one thing then do another, you're being *incongruent* (though not necessarily acting without integrity).

When I was married, I remember my wife telling me about the new diet she started. She was so excited. She found the website, really appreciated the teacher's point of view, joined the group, and got into the program. A couple weeks went by, and I asked her how the program was going and if she was still just as excited about it.

She asked, "What program?"

I said, "That food program you started a couple weeks back."

She said, "Oh, that? I quit that about a week ago. It wasn't for me."

"Oh."

She had a right to change her mind, of course, but she would start and stop things so often that I couldn't tell what was still true and valid and what wasn't. She'd say one thing then do another, which confused and many times frustrated me. It started to put a strain on our relationship.

Her behavior was not the downfall of our marriage, but it made me trust her less and less. When you're incongruent, people around you pick up on it. Not only will they find it hard to trust you, but you'll have difficulty trusting yourself too—and not just in the context of relationships.

HOW YOU SHOW UP DETERMINES HOW YOUR LIFE TURNS OUT

If you often commit to things but don't follow through, you may find that you never seem to get anything done. You might even ask yourself why nothing in your life ever seems to work out. It's like going to the gas station, removing the gas cap, driving off without filling your tank, then wondering why your gas gauge still reads empty.

Not following through on the commitments that you make to yourself will cause you to start developing self-doubt and fears, but you won't know why. You'll trust your instincts less and less and will begin questioning your own decisions.

Because your subconscious mind believes everything you tell it, it responds to you as if you are speaking the truth. It will set things in motion and get ready for you to follow through on your commitments. But when you change course and set sail in another direction, the subconscious mind gets confused and has to recalibrate in order to adapt to the new course. And since the subconscious mind is the foundation of all your behavior, the more you confuse it the more you will notice yourself doing things that surprise and even disappoint you.

Indecisiveness and lack of confidence develop when you keep feeding your subconscious mind false information. The more you commit to something then break that commitment, the more *incongruent* you become inside, and you actually start creating your own chaos!

You'll find it hard to get anywhere in the outer world because your inner world is in disarray. If you keep breaking promises to yourself, it will get harder to trust your own judgment and you'll find yourself making the wrong decisions more often than not. You might even find that "bad luck" seems to follow you everywhere you go. The truth is, the subconscious mind is a well-oiled machine that works fine on its own until we feed it something that sludges up the gears.

WHAT ARE YOU FEEDING YOUR SUBCONSCIOUS MIND?

One thing you don't want to feed it is mixed signals. Incongruent thoughts and behavior mixes up the data going to your brain and creates dysfunction.

Your behavior is how you "show up" in the world. So, how do you show up? Do you follow through with your commitments to yourself?

I remember when I was married and my wife brought home a dog. *I did not want a dog.* But she found him on a rescue site online and *had* to have him. So we became the owners of a 3-year-old Pomeranian named Balonee (yes, we named him Balonee).

Balonee loved my wife but could barely tolerate me. And even though I didn't want him in the first place, I made the commitment to take care of him as best I could. I did everything the trainer taught me to do and even researched more ways to have a healthy relationship with a dog.

Over time, Balonee developed respect for me and saw me as the "pack leader." However, there was a point when he was simply too much to handle. We had fallen on hard times, and taking care of ourselves, let alone a dog, was challenging enough.

So my wife came up with the idea of giving him to a home that could love and support him. As convenient as that would have been for both of us, I had already made the commitment to take care of Balonee for as long as he was alive. In fact, I had made this commitment a long time ago, before I ever met my wife.

When I was in my twenties, I took my two cats to the Humane Society because I felt like I couldn't handle them anymore. They were peeing in the house, and I was too young and naive to learn how to properly care for them. I was also not compassionate enough to care about what happened to them. I remember the day I dropped them off, looking back over my shoulder as I walked out the door to see their faces one last time. Back then, I just wanted to get rid of them. They were a nuisance and all I cared about were my clean carpets. I was more interested in myself and my own needs than theirs, and I didn't really care about pets. I never found out if they were adopted or not.

After several years, when I had grown older and more mature, I was suddenly struck with guilt and sadness for what I had done. By this time, I had also developed more compassion for animals, and understood that they experience fear, joy, and other emotions just like we do. That realization made me sink into the worst feeling imaginable.

The guilt, sadness, remorse, and other heavy emotions hit me hard as I processed that event in my life for the first time. In fact, now that they were gone, I thought that I would have to live with that guilt for the rest of my life. There was absolutely no way to take back what I had done.

Eventually, I found a way to help alleviate some of the guilt. I realized there was no way to change the past, but a thought came to mind: "If

I can't make it up to them, I can at least learn from my experience and make sure I give all of the other animals in my life the best possible existence I can."

This brought me some peace. If I am able to be a caring, compassionate, and committed person to the other animals I have now and in the future, then that is something I can feel good about. I made a promise that I have kept to this day. I swore that I would never abandon any of my pets ever again. I made a commitment that I would do whatever it took to care for them in the best possible way for as long as they live.

And I've held on to that commitment ever since. It hasn't always been easy, but it has been rewarding. Not only because the animals in my life get treated very well, but also because I became very clear in what I needed to do and who I am in that area of my life now.

When my wife commented that we should find our dog Balonee a new home, I spoke without hesitation. "Absolutely not. I will not put him through that. I will take care of him for the rest of his life." And I followed through with that commitment. Then, when we got divorced, Balonee left with her and I never saw him again. But I kept my promise to him to the best of my ability and did whatever I could to make sure he had a comfortable life as long as we were together.

Do you follow through with commitments to yourself? Your answer will very likely have a direct correlation with the results you're getting in life. When you are more congruent on the inside, your life usually turns out the way you plan. Not always, of course, as challenges will arise that seem to test you at every corner. But even when there are surprises, you are much better prepared to handle them if you have a good relationship with your subconscious mind.

CONGRUENCE: BUILDING A STRONG FOUNDATION OF SELF-TRUST

The more you follow through with your intentions, the more in alignment you'll be with *everything* in your life. In other words, when you behave as you intend to behave, you'll be more prepared when things go bad. And things will go bad! So it's important to figure out where you aren't following through with the commitments you make to yourself. Even small commitments that you think aren't that important add up, causing chaos down the road.

If you truly want to "show up" in the best way possible and set yourself up for success, learning to be more congruent in your behavior is a great first step. The small steps you take toward fulfilling your own commitments create a compound effect and build a strong foundation of trust in yourself.

Think of the things you might say on a typical day but may not follow through on:

➡ Tomorrow, I'm going to the gym.

➡ I'm going to volunteer.

➡ I'll be leaving in a few minutes.

➡ I'll wash the dishes later.

➡ I'll call you tonight.

Any item on this list may not be important by itself if you fail to follow through with it, but a repeated pattern of unfulfilled commitments over time, even with seemingly mundane tasks, builds *distrust* in yourself. The shift is subtle, because it can happen over months or years. But as you break these small self-commitments, you become less confident and more hesitant in your decision-making process.

Good decision-makers are those that make a commitment and take action on that commitment, even if they aren't 100 percent sure of the outcome. That doesn't mean they're always right about the decisions they make, but they learn fast. They also build a wealth of references along the way so they learn what works and what doesn't, causing decision-making to be easier in the future. The more you succeed *and* fail, the faster you learn what works.

Something else that is just as important as honoring self-commitments is being in integrity with what you value most in life. Your values—the stuff that's most important to you—are what motivate you and drive your behavior at an even deeper level than what I've already talked about in this chapter.

Being in congruence helps you prepare for the hard stuff in life by making sure your behavior aligns with your intentions, but *motivation* influences those intentions inside of you.

> **Motivation is the driving force of your actions, and whatever you value most in life will be what determines the decisions you make. However, if you are not absolutely sure about what you value most, you may be making decisions that don't serve you.**

For example, I used to value a high wage over anything else when it came to work. I would decide whether a job was worth pursuing based almost exclusively on the pay. After I got hired, I would soon reach a burnout point and decide to quit. Time after time, each job wouldn't work out for one reason or another. When I stopped focusing on the money and started looking for work where my input was respected, my success and happiness level at work improved. For the first time, I actually enjoyed my job. And the more I enjoyed it, the harder I worked at it and the faster I received raises and promotions.

I had to figure out what I really valued most about having a career. Was money so important that it was the deciding factor that made a job great? Or was there something I was missing, causing me to sabotage my longevity at any job? I decided to write down what my ideal job would look like. I asked myself, "What would make a job great?"

I created a list. On that list was what I wanted most in a job, like respect from my coworkers and superiors, pleasure in what I do, weekends off, the ability to leave work at work, good pay, and more. However, instead of just looking for all of these things in a job, I placed each item in order of priority from most important to least important. What I came up with was what changed everything. Knowing what I would absolutely not budge on and what I could be more flexible with determined how long I lasted in a job. And I noticed that when I chose to stay in alignment with what I valued most, I was always happier at what I was doing.

When you are not getting the results you want or are not as happy as you could be in any area of life, the reason may be that you are unsure about what you value most. Learning what your values are will make your path clear, so let's figure those out next.

CHAPTER 2
Stopping Self-Sabotage

If you are not in alignment with what you value most in life, you will find yourself more unhappy and likely to do behavior that ends up causing you more harm than good.

This self-sabotaging behavior can come in the form of bad relationships, bad careers, and other challenges in the major areas of your life. And just like I mentioned in the last chapter, you might even find that after years of doing things that fail over and over again, you no longer trust your own decisions.

One example of that is a person who keeps getting into bad relationships. They meet someone that seems nice, but later on find out their new partner is controlling and abusive. So they break it off, grateful to be out of that situation. Then, when they're ready to date again, they get into yet another relationship with someone else who has the same character flaws as the last one!

One of the main reasons this might happen is because you will always attract and be attracted to people who are at a similar level of dysfunction as you (we'll talk more about this concept in Chapter 6).

Jude: A Setup for Failed Relationships

I once met a woman (I'll call her Jude) who said she wanted to be with someone who "took care of her for once in her life." Jude was used to being the one who made the money and took charge in the relationship, so she wanted a change. Her boyfriends over the years were somewhat timid and somewhat broke, and they thoroughly enjoyed being supported and taken care of. A relationship like this can work if that's what both people want, but Jude wanted someone else to take care of things once in a while.

Jude would only seek potential partners that were "very nice," "super sweet," and accommodating. She thought that if she found someone like that, she could relax into her femininity more and not have to stress about so many things all the time. What she found out over and over again, however, was that the more passive and sweet the guys were, the less likely they were to stand up for themselves or handle challenging situations. Because of that, Jude felt as if she had no choice but to step in and take on a more masculine role (and identity) in order to get things done in her relationships.

Jude thought she wanted a sensitive, caring, sympathetic, and passive partner. But that turned out to be exactly what kept her unhappy. She would always end up in relationships with men that were too needy, got stressed out really fast, and didn't want to deal with conflict.

Her dysfunctions *complemented* her typical partner's dysfunctions, which is the reason why she kept attracting the same type of people over and over again. Her high need to control outcomes, her aggressive personality, and her fears about never having enough money subconsciously drove her to seek men who were usually passive and easygoing and not really concerned about making a lot of (or any) money.

What Jude was trying to accomplish in her relationships would always come crashing down on her because she didn't realize that she felt most comfortable being who she'd always been. She was setting herself up for failure over and over again. Jude's behavior was being driven by some unscrutinized and perhaps even unknown values that were guiding her most of her life.

This is what happens in many relationships that don't work out. We can be motivated by deep, core-level values that may not apply in our world today. And when you find yourself in bad situations over and over again, it's time to revisit and reevaluate those values so that you can end that unnecessary cycle.

WHY YOU DO WHAT YOU DO

Values are what motivate your behavior. They are the primary drivers behind what you do and why you do it.

Jude thought she needed to find a man that was soft and gentle because she believed it would allow her to be more relaxed in her femininity. For so long, she had held on to a more masculine role where she was used to taking action, taking control, and being more authoritative. She believed that if neither she nor her partner embraced some masculinity, nothing would ever get done, so she felt the need to step up and take charge. She had consistently sought men that avoided conflict and were too laid back, which may have played a primary role in sabotaging her relationships.

Jude used criteria that she set up a long time ago that defined for her what a "good" relationship is. That set of values motivated her to make the choices she was making, giving her the results she didn't want. If you can't figure out why you keep getting the same, unwanted results, you may be unconsciously setting yourself up for failure. After you complete the exercise Discover What's Most Important to You (page 17), you'll learn what you value most and how it might be determining your path.

Your Values Are the Rules for Your Life

Values are rules and guidelines that will determine your outcome almost every time, unless you choose to deviate from those values.

That's when things get interesting.

You have every right to alter your course and go against one or more of your values. However, if that's something you find yourself doing often, you may want to update them to help you create *new* behavior that serves you. When you do behavior that serves you, it can become a valuable behavior to repeat and eventually transform into a new rule or guideline in your life. And when you are in alignment with the guidelines you create for yourself, you almost always live a happier, more fulfilling existence. But the trick is to stay in alignment, otherwise the path can become littered with obstacles.

Aligning with values that serve you is a *very powerful* way to create the life you want. That's why it's so important to know what your values are so that you understand what's driving your behavior.

Do You Know Your Values?

You probably know exactly what's important to you in almost all the major areas of your life. You've lived long enough to realize what you do and don't want, and you likely do your best to keep those things in mind as you get into new relationships, new careers, and other major life situations. That way you can lead a somewhat normal, and even enjoyable, existence. In relationships, you probably prefer an honest, respectful partner. In careers, you might value friendly coworkers. But what about wants and desires that aren't being met? Are you living by values that you don't even know exist?

When you are succeeding in one area of life but not doing so well in another, you will almost always discover values you weren't aware of deeply ingrained in you. These values motivate you to make decisions that will either be healthy or unhealthy for you. When you live by values that aren't healthy for you, it's like driving along the road of life wearing a blindfold, hoping you don't hit anything along the way. The biggest challenge is trying to figure out just what those underlying values are before you veer off course too far.

For example, if one of your values in personal health and wellness is to maintain a certain weight but you continue eating foods that cause weight gain, you probably have underlying values that override your intention. That might mean deep down you value eating junk food more than getting to that ideal weight. It's not that you're broken or even wrong, it just means that somewhere along the way you prioritized one behavior over another and made it stick. These hidden or unknown values can cause so much havoc! You can have the best intentions but still do things that sabotage your journey of healing and growth.

You can also have values that directly conflict with each other and until you address those conflicts, your problems may never go away. Your values may be so deeply ingrained that the resulting obstacles might seem impossible to avoid. Valuing eating junk food over maintaining a healthy weight is the perfect example of this. Both values may be very important to you (yes, enjoying junk food can be a value), but there is definitely a conflict between them that will set you up for failure.

In Jude's case, she may have had a value that stated, "I must feel secure in my relationships." But if her new partner was timid and preferred no conflicts, she would find herself taking charge more often than not, stifling that feeling of security. She wanted to be able to trust that her partner could take care of things so that she didn't have to feel like she needed to be in control all the time. Even though she dated nice guys, many of them were not capable of giving her what she needed. It's possible that she was holding on to values that no longer served her. This may be because of something she hasn't been able to let go of from her past (i.e., a bad relationship), or a belief that she developed that may no longer be true.

> **When you know what you value most, you will always know the right path to take.**

If you are still carrying around old emotional pain or beliefs that no longer apply, you may be holding on to values that you don't need. The beliefs you created as a child typically aren't applicable in the adult world and in fact may be causing you a lot of strife today. So let me help you get very clear on what you value most in the major areas of your life. Once you have clarity on your values, you can use them as a beacon to help you make decisions that are right for you.

The following exercise will help you stop self-sabotage and get you to a congruent place inside you where you achieve the outcomes you want.

||||EXERCISE ||||||||||||||||||||||||||||||||||||||||||||||||||||||||||||||||||||||||||||||||||||||||||||||||||||||

Discover What's Most Important to You

If you are currently making decisions that are not in your highest interest or in alignment with what's most important to you, *you will almost always end up with failure.*

This exercise walks you through the process of discovering what you value most so that you can understand why you behave and respond the way you do in specific areas of your life. It's also a great way to learn how to prevent future chaos!

I'm going to ask you a series of questions that will help you determine what your highest values are in all of the major areas of your life, or at least the ones you feel need the most attention. This somewhat simple process will reveal some powerful results to help you begin to shape your future the way you want.

For example, if your relationships are suffering but you're doing great in your career, it may be better to focus on relationships first. You don't necessarily need to explore your values in areas that are already a success in your life.

Got your pen and paper ready? This is a very effective and enlightening exercise, so don't just breeze past it. If you follow through with this, you will experience some significant improvements in the area of your life you're working on. For this process, all you need to do is come up with single words or phrases. All the answers you come up with are the right answers because they are yours.

Also, make sure you only write down what your values are today, not what you want them to be. And, yes, you'll have an opportunity to change them if they don't serve you.

BRAIN RESET

Every now and then during this exercise, I'm going to ask you to clear your mind to help you "reset" your brain before moving on to certain questions. This will put you in the best state possible for getting the most accurate answers.

To begin, clear your mind and think about what you like to do on vacation.

Got that vacation in mind? *Really feel like you're there…*

When you're ready, come back to now and answer question number 1.

1. **Write a number of priority next to each of the following major life areas.**

Mark a 1 next to the area that needs the most attention, a 2 on the one that needs a little less, and so on. If you find some have an equal ranking, just prioritize one over the other for now. You can always redo this step later. Prioritizing the areas helps you figure out which ones you need to focus on first.

____ Relationships

____ Work and Career

____ Physical Health

____ Mental and Emotional Health

____ Family

____ Spirituality

____ Other: _____

2. **Answer the question, "What is important to me about what I placed in position number 1?"**

For example, if you placed Work and Career in position number 1, you would answer the question, "What is important to me about Work and Career?"

Here are some sample answers to this question:

1. I have to get along with my coworkers.

2. My job must be close to home.

3. I want to stay busy.

4. I want free time.

5. I want an easygoing boss.

6. I must work for an ethical company.

7. There has to be plenty of air conditioning.

8. I want to make good money.

9. I don't want to work over 40 hours a week.

10. I want weekends off.

This list could go on for quite a while, but you get the idea.

Write down every word or phrase that comes to mind. Try to come up with at least 10 items, but don't stop writing if you can come up with more.

_____

_____

_____

_____

_____

_____

_____

_____

_____

_____

When you can't think of any more, move on to the next question.

⟋BRAIN RESET

Now that you've come up with a list of what's important to you, think of what you love to do while you're on vacation. And if vacations aren't your thing, just imagine doing something you really enjoy. Got it in mind? Great. Enjoy that for a moment, then come back to now, and let's continue.

3. What else is important to you about your position number 1 answer?

That's right, just when you thought you were done! It's a similar question as before, but by exploring it again after resetting your brain, you'll be able to dig a little deeper into your mind and find that you can probably come up with more.

Really dig in and let whatever comes up, come up.

_____

_____

_____

_____

_____

⟋BRAIN RESET

You're doing great! Ready for another reset?

Remember that thing you really enjoy? Are there any sounds where you are in your mind? Are there any colors? What stands out? Sit with that image for just a few seconds or longer. Really embrace it and breathe it in. If you have any trouble visualizing, just focus on the feelings.

Good, come back to now when you're ready. We're getting closer to some real results here.

4. This is the last time I'm going to ask, I promise: What *else* is important to you about your answer in position number 1?

The reason I'm asking you this question one more time is because it will help you dive deep into your subconscious mind. This is where some well-established core values may be buried. After a couple of brain resets, the deeper stuff can often float to the surface.

If you can't think of anything else, just move on to the next step. Otherwise, write down what comes up for you.

_____

_____

_____

_____

_____

5. Arrange all your values in order of *most important* to *least important*.

There will be a lot of words moving on this step, so it's handy to do this on a computer.

The easiest way to do this is to compare the first value with the second value and ask yourself: Is value 1 more important than value 2?

Using an excerpt from the previous example list on Work and Career, notice how I've arranged all the values in a certain order. What you want to end up with is a list showing the most important values to least important, starting at number 1. Since your first attempt at this list will likely not be in the right order, this is where you'll get a chance to rearrange it any way you'd like.

Sample Values for Work and Career

1. I have to get along with my coworkers.

2. My job must be close to home.

3. I want to stay busy.

4. I want free time.

5. I want an easygoing boss.

6. I want weekends off.

Using this list as an example, your comparison question would be:

Is getting along with my coworkers more important than my job being close to home? If you answer yes, the order doesn't change, so go on to the next comparison.

(value 1 to value 3): Is getting along with my coworkers more important than staying busy? Repeat this process until you get a no. When and if you do, swap the value order and start again.

For this example, I'm going to say, getting along with my coworkers is not more important than staying busy, so I moved staying busy up to position number 1 and moved getting along with my coworkers to position number 2:

1. I want to stay busy.
2. I have to get along with my coworkers.
3. My job must be close to home.
4. I want free time.
5. I want an easygoing boss.
6. I want weekends off.

If this seems a bit complicated, just remember all you're doing is placing them in order of importance. Position number 1 will always be the most important value, position number 2 the second, and so on. Make your comparisons by testing if 1 is more important than 2, if 2 is more important than 3, and so on.

When you are done, you will end up with a list that shows you what's most important at the top, and what's least important toward the bottom. Your list will likely be bigger than this example, but you get the idea.

If you run into some values that you feel are about equal in importance, just combine them (i.e., a value of "fun" and a value of "enjoyment" might be the same for you, so just combine them into one value: "fun and enjoyment").

If you have difficulty prioritizing one value over another, just ask yourself this question:

If I had A, would that give me B?

In other words, if you couldn't decide if free time was more important than having weekends, ask yourself:

If I had free time, would that give me weekends off?

Or reverse it:

If I had weekends off, would that give me free time?

Whatever you answer "yes" to becomes the more important value.

In this example, my answer to "If I had weekends off, would that give me free time?" would be "yes," so I would put weekends off higher on my values list than free time.

Why You Make the Decisions You Do

Once you are done moving your values around, you'll have a pretty solid list of what you value most in that area of life, in order from most important (number 1) to least important.

If you want to know what motivates you to make the decisions you make and do the behaviors you do, the answer lies in your top five values:

⇒ Values 1 and 2 are ones that you absolutely can't live without. These are the primary drivers that motivate you over everything else.

⇒ Values 3 and 4 are those that you *must* have, but you may be flexible about them on occasion for various reasons. But if you don't honor them the *majority* of the time, you will not be as fulfilled as you could be.

⇒ Value 5 is also important but has a little less impact on your behavior. It is still a primary component in your

decision-making process, but not in the same way as values
1 through 4.

Some people absolutely honor all five of their values and won't take anything less. These people are extremely motivated to make life work *for* them. They will not settle and they always make decisions that are in alignment with those values no matter what.

It's really up to you how much you want to enforce and honor your values. What I've found is that the more you regard your highest values, the more fulfilling and stress free your life will be.

For example, if your highest value in relationships is safety, and you decide to get into a relationship with someone who makes you feel unsafe, you will never be satisfied in that relationship. Being in a relationship with someone who does not fall into alignment with your values can be a good indicator that the relationship won't last.

Making decisions outside of your values creates fear and sometimes resentment inside of you. You think you're happy, but there's always *something* that's just not right. It's that something that could be a direct violation of one of your values.

When you violate your own values, you become a victim and start blaming the world for your problems. You'll say or think things like, "She should know not to do that to me," or "Doesn't he realize I don't like that?" What's really happening when you don't honor your values is that you are actually inviting chaos into your life. You think that other people should know better and that they should stop their behavior toward you. However, it's really up to you to do or say something to let others know where you stand. And if others choose not to honor your values after that, you need to take steps to get out of those situations. By discovering and honoring your values, you will know exactly where you stand and your life will improve dramatically.

In other words, there will never be a question of "What should I do?" or "Which decision is the right one?" because all you need is to make sure your decision is in alignment with your values.

If you want to know exactly how to do that, go on to the final step of this process.

6. Weigh every important decision or behavior against your highest values.

If you really want to avoid self-sabotage, start asking yourself the following question when faced with major decisions in your life:

Is this decision in alignment with my highest values?

If you answer no, seriously reconsider your decision. If you choose to forge ahead anyway, moving against your values, you will end up creating a conflict inside of you, which will weigh you down.

CONFLICT CREATES RESISTANCE

Whenever you make a decision against your highest values, you create resistance in your mind and body. Think of resistance as a blockage of the flow of thoughts and emotions. I realize this is a little bit of "out there" thinking, but if you examine this concept in terms of happiness being a free-flowing emotional state as opposed to unhappiness, which feels more slow and prodding, you might get an image of what I'm referring to.

If you put a kink in a water hose, that creates resistance and builds pressure in the hose. The mind and body work that way too. If you are out of alignment with your values, it's like putting a kink in your system. You will feel the resistance and the pressure will build. The pressure comes from the conflict between your intentions and actions. When your intention is to honor your values but your actions show otherwise, you create a conflict inside of you. This conflict is a consistent reminder that you may have made the wrong choice.

You know the feeling you get after you regret a decision, right? It's the same feeling you get when conflict arises in you. Being in conflict with your values can certainly cause havoc, but if life still seems harder than it "should" be, it may be time to reevaluate your values and find out if they are still serving you. Your values can change. In fact, if you discover that a value is no longer important to you, you can replace it with a different one! Sometimes you go through life and figure out that what was once important isn't so important anymore.

If you discover something that's important to you, simply slip it into your values list where it fits best. Put that new value in the order that makes the most sense to you.

Values ebb and flow throughout life so you never have to stick with ones that don't serve you anymore. But when you honor the ones that do serve you, you create a very rewarding and enriching life.

If you ever find it challenging to honor your values because it might mean sacrificing something else in your life, the sacrifice might not be as bad as you think. For example, one of my highest values in intimate relationships is respect. If my romantic partner doesn't respect me, that can be a deal breaker no matter how much in love I am. It doesn't mean I break it off right then and there, as there will always be open discussion about an issue, but it does go to show how much I follow through with honoring my values.

You will also run into situations when you can relax on your values a bit too. Just feel those situations out. In my case, if it turned out my romantic partner disrespected me because of a misunderstanding, I would certainly be more lenient in enforcing my values.

The final thing I want to mention about values is that you may discover a once high-level value that doesn't apply any longer. If that's the case, simply let it go. Take it off your list and remove it from your mind. Just like Jude, who may no longer need to seek that secure feeling, but can instead focus on other values that will help her create the life she wants. After a few years of dating people that allow her to feel secure, Jude may develop trust in her own decision-making process and decide that *security* is no longer something she needs to think about anymore. She doesn't have to think about finding certain kinds of partners because good decisions about potential partners come naturally now. She may still have that value on her list somewhere, but it can move down where it isn't as much of a priority anymore.

WHEN A VALUE BECOMES A PART OF YOU

When a value gets met time and time again, it becomes a part of who you are. It no longer has to be high on your list of things to remember because there is no doubt you will always have it. A good example of that is a person who's been poor his entire life then suddenly becomes wealthy. His highest value in Work and Career might have been making more money, but now that he has lots of it, there's no need for him to keep it as a value anymore. He no longer has to ask himself if his decisions are in alignment with making more money (unless he wants to make even more money than he currently is, in which case that value could stay put).

Your values are deep-seated programs running in the background of your mind. When you go against them, you set yourself up for failure time and time again.

When I wrote out my values for Work and Career, I started getting work that I actually enjoyed instead of work that drained my soul. I even quit jobs that I absolutely needed because they fell out of alignment with my values. That created some very scary moments, but in the end, my decisions to honor my values always worked out for the best.

Every time you honor your values, you gain more confidence in yourself and your decision-making process. The "honoring" part can be the hardest thing to do, however. If you're used to making decisions based on how other people respond to you, you are living life from a place of fear, not empowerment.

In order to start feeling empowered, you want to make decisions based on what's in your best interest. Learning to honor yourself in every way is the most important step in the personal empowerment process.

Honoring your values begins the process of aligning your intentions with your behavior (congruence). Once you are aligned, you will feel more confident and you'll find that you get more of what you want in life instead of what you don't want.

Aligning with your values creates a great foundation, but honoring your personal boundaries goes one giant step further by revealing your authenticity, and telling the world what you will and won't accept in your life. Once you're comfortable being fully authentic, you no longer have to hide who you really are inside.

Would you like to show up as your authentic self without fear? Let's talk about honoring your personal boundaries next.

CHAPTER 3
Why You're Not Getting the Results You Want

YOU HAVE A CHOICE

Back in 1995, I quit my job working for an alarm company. I was the assistant manager for a large department of 24 employees and was on call 24 hours a day. Anytime, day or night, I was available to support the company, the staff, and our clients. Back then we used pagers, and frequently I'd feel a vibration coming from my hip.

To this day, I still remember the number that flashed on the screen. Like always, I'd grab my bulky nineties cell phone and call the office to find out what they needed. It was rare that I wasn't able to resolve the problem right away. I was efficient because I experienced almost every type of challenge and subsequently learned what it took to resolve them.

But being on call was wearing on me. After about four years at the same job, where I was getting paged while I was eating, at the movies, or even in bed sound asleep, even my free time wasn't free anymore. I reached a burnout point, so I had to do something or I'd go insane. I chose to quit.

After I gave my resignation, I was told to walk over and speak to the general manager of the company to finalize things. I arrived at his office and sat down in the chair in front of his desk, and he asked me a question I didn't expect: "Is there anything we can do that would make you want to stay?"

I thought, "Wow, I didn't expect that question!" Actually, I didn't know what to expect but I knew for sure that I was ready to leave. In fact, I felt so confident in my decision, I wasn't nervous in the slightest as I might have been at any other job. Probably because this was the first job that wore me down to the point of exhaustion, and I was reaching critical mass knowing that I was about to have a breakdown.

Making the decision to quit *no matter what* was what really got me focused on tending to my own needs for the first time in a long time. For once since my first day on the job, my thoughts were aligned with my feelings and my actions were in alignment with my thoughts. In other words, I was completely congruent. I became certain, assertive, and very aware of the path I needed to take.

The general manager's question surprised me because I never realized I actually had a *choice* in changing my circumstances. I didn't know it was an option! That moment both empowered me and depressed me at the same time. I never considered asking for what I wanted from my employers because I believed that they would just fire me if I showed anything less than complete satisfaction in my job. And there I was in the general manager's office giving my notice, after four years of obediently doing what I was told to do. Never before did I realize that he actually cared about what *I* wanted for *me*.

That event made an impact on me. It wasn't often that I spoke up about what I wanted or what bothered me at work. I never gave anyone a chance to fulfill my wants or needs because I thought I wasn't in a position to ask. I was on call every day and I never shared with my superiors that I needed a break from time to time. I was too scared that any deviation from their expectations would either show up on my next evaluation or cause them to terminate me.

All those years went by draining my motivation and energy day after day, and I never thought to speak up for myself. I chose to quit because I didn't think speaking up was an option.

HOW HAPPINESS ERODES

Have you ever chosen not to speak up for yourself simply because you didn't think it was an option? Had I spoken up to my boss and asked for what I wanted months or even years earlier, the company might have actually made changes to accommodate me. And it's possible I would have stayed working for them because of it.

Instead, I spoke to no one about my gripes and just made the decision to quit when I reached burnout. I didn't realize I was letting my personal boundaries get crossed slowly over time, causing me to distance myself from people. The joy I used to get from my work was disintegrating and no one knew about it. My employer never got the chance to make things right for me because I never gave them the option; I just made the decision to quit one day. I'd had enough.

Honoring your personal boundaries isn't only about not letting others walk all over you or violate your personal space; it's also about protecting yourself so that you aren't emotionally drained or taken advantage of. When you don't honor yourself, your happiness erodes over time without your even realizing it. It slowly fades and you become more and more jaded.

However, when you're able to express yourself and make it known to the people in your life what you will or won't allow, expressing to them which behavior is okay and which is not, they will clearly see what you need them to do to honor your honoring yourself.

One of the underlying philosophies of my coaching and *The Over-whelmed Brain* podcast is that when you honor yourself, you tend to get the results you want in life as opposed to the ones you don't. The more your behavior aligns with your thoughts and feelings, the more authenticity you are putting out into the world. When you are being authentically you, you are less stressed, more motivated, and taking bolder steps to create the outcomes you want. *You're simply happier.*

Personal boundaries are directly related to the level of respect you have for yourself. The more you respect yourself, the more you'll be able to honor your path even if others disagree with you. The hard part is honoring yourself no matter what the consequences. That doesn't mean you do anything you want, anytime you want, but it does mean you take into account what's right for you first and fore-most before honoring what's right for others.

There are exceptions to that rule, of course, but this chapter is focused on considering yourself first so that you have enough to give to others without losing a part of yourself in the process.

You are worthy and deserve respect.

So give that respect to yourself and you'll soon find that you are cre-ating more freedom and less strife. On top of that, you'll discover you are much less resentful of the behavior of others. Why? Because other people feed off of how we "show up" in the world. We all feed off of the behavior of other people. And if we let others walk on us, it's not always necessarily something they are doing intentionally. They are just feeding off of the part of our personality we are allowing to come through.

Much of life's resentments come from the inability or choice to not honor our boundaries. The more we choose not to stand up or speak up for ourselves, the more resentful we get of others.

> **We create self-perpetuating resentment and anger toward others by not expressing what we truly want from them.**

We assume other people know what we want, then wait for them to accommodate us in some way. This is especially prevalent in familial or intimate relationships. When you are with someone for a long time, you think you know them well. You believe you know what they're thinking and what they feel inside. However, how often do the close people in your life not "get" you?

How often have others thought they knew how you felt, but they were wrong? That's probably one of the largest causes of miscommunication in the world today. We may know how someone will respond in certain situations, but we rarely know exactly what they're feeling or thinking inside. That's why it's so important to be genuine and expressive with others so that they know what you need or expect from them.

A great example of that is when I was married. For almost eight years, I was extremely judgmental of my wife. In my mind, she could rarely do anything "right," and I made sure to point out all her faults. Year after year, our relationship was disintegrating but I didn't know it. I just believed that we were always a "work in progress." I couldn't see that we weren't progressing at all.

I was afraid to be truthful with her for fear that she might leave or get upset with me. I had the same type of fear in many other life situations as well. I would often not speak up and tell people what I really wanted because I believed the consequences would not be favorable. So, in order to get what I wanted, I was covert about my wants and needs. I communicated in a passive-aggressive way, giving subtle clues about what I wanted instead of clear, direct messages. This brought a lot of misunderstanding and miscommunication, and also created a lot of resentment in me because "if they cared, they should already know what I want."

I never shared with my wife what would make me happy. Instead, I tried to change her behavior to accommodate me. This is a vicious cycle that many couples do without knowing they're doing it. When you are unhappy about something in your partner, you may want *them* to change instead of healing a part of yourself. This is exactly how the relationship with my wife went for the entire eight years we were together. I figured the only way to keep her, or any intimate partner in my life, was to not tell them the whole truth. After all, "If they knew the real me, they would leave me."

This kind of thinking drove a wedge in my marriage and every other relationship I'd ever had. The choice I made to not speak my truth caused my partners in life to guess at what I was feeling and thinking because I never spoke up. My wife spent eight years trying to please me because she had no idea what I really wanted. Had she not left the marriage, we might still be buried in that dysfunction today.

When you don't speak your truth, you leave space for other people to make up their own stories about you. The less I shared with my wife, the more unanswered questions she had about me. And even when she asked those questions, she rarely got honest answers because I was afraid of how she would respond if she knew the truth. I made sure I never revealed my true thoughts to her, which created a false reality for both of us.

When you choose to hide what you think and feel, you cut people out of your life without even trying. I chose to hide my true thoughts in my relationships and because of that, my partners never knew the real me. It became a guessing game that they could never win. This created a struggle that was nearly impossible for either of us to identify, mainly because neither of us showed up as ourselves.

If you don't share who you are and what you want, how will you ever form lasting bonds with anyone? They'll never know the real you and you'll never feel completely connected, plus you'll be missing the chance to feel the freedom of being yourself.

SELF-COMPASSION BEFORE COMPASSION FOR OTHERS

One of the most common misconceptions when it comes to honoring your boundaries is believing other people will be upset when you do. You think they won't like you anymore or they'll be unhappy that you don't submit to their wants and needs as you may have done in the past.

There are people in your life that won't like when you honor your own needs first because they've gotten comfortable with who you've been. And if you're the type of person who typically honors other people's wants and needs before your own, it can create a deficit in you. You can feel like you are being taken advantage of, as if those other people don't care how you feel as long as their needs are getting met.

Avoiding Emotional Deficit

This may sound harsh, but if you really want to have more authentic, fulfilling relationships, do not be kind, compassionate, or generous to those around you at the cost of your own well-being. You can only do this for so long before you burn out and become resentful.

We are often taught to show selfless compassion to others, but this can be unhealthy in many circumstances. There are times to show selfless compassion for sure, like running into a burning building to save a kitten. However, if you make a habit of exhibiting selfless compassion in everyday circumstances, it will wear you out and you will end up in emotional deficit. You will have given so much that you will no longer be able to come from a compassionate place.

Honoring others over yourself is like dishonoring yourself.

Compassion starts on the inside, and when you have enough of it for yourself, only then can you spread it out into the world for others. When you aren't compassionate to yourself first, what you give to others is not really compassion at all. You cannot give compassion without coming from a place of self-compassion first.

The more compassionate you are to yourself, the more compassion you will have to give to others. You can develop more self-compassion by asking the question: "Before I give to anyone else, what do I need first and foremost for myself?" Follow through on your answer because it will be one of the most important first steps to a healthier you and healthier relationships.

If you're a people-pleaser and just want to make sure everyone's happy all the time, you may find yourself getting worn out trying to keep up with the demand. People-pleasers tend to give and give until they are so tired they feel empty inside. They may believe that they are doing the right thing by making others happy, but they don't give enough to themselves to keep the balance they need to enjoy life.

I used to think my own happiness came from pleasing those around me without worrying about my own wants or needs. I figured that as long as those around me were happy, they were more likely to reciprocate—then I'd be happy too. But more often than not, they did *not* give back us much as I gave to them, if at all. This caused me to lose many relationships, both intimate and platonic, because I got tired of giving all the time. I would even put the blame on them for not giving back, instead of looking at myself for not being more authentic and expressive.

The only way others will know what you want is when you are authentic and speak your truth. Don't expect others to guess and then hope they get it right. Everyone is wired differently and too few know what others want unless they're good at asking questions.

Ask yourself questions. Determine what you need, and honor yourself first. This sounds selfish, I realize, but what you end up doing is fulfilling your needs so that you aren't giving to others from a place of lack. Giving or loving from lack is not really giving or loving at all! It's dysfunction. You can't care for others if you aren't taking care of yourself, because soon you'll have nothing left in you to give.

When compassion for others doesn't come from compassion for yourself first, it's not really compassion at all; it's sacrifice. And when you do that more often than not, you are stripping away your spirit and happiness day by day. Self-compassion has to come first or you will have nothing more to give.

You can show compassion to yourself by honoring those boundaries I talked about earlier. Treat yourself as if you were a child that you were assigned to protect. That sounds a little strange, but I'll explain it in a moment. Your personal boundaries are your castle walls, and by letting the wrong people in, you risk being overrun and overpowered. When that happens, happiness starts to fade away.

Protecting yourself as if you were a child is part of a powerful process of honoring yourself to the fullest. I've presented a great example of this on my show a few times:

> Imagine you are standing 20 feet from a small child on the sidewalk. The child's back is facing you and he or she is facing the street. A van pulls up in front of the child and one of the side doors open. You can tell that the child doesn't

know who these people are, but they are smiling and seem friendly enough.

One of the men in the van motions for the child to get in, and you can see the child shake their head "no." The child, clearly distressed, starts to look around to find out if anyone else is nearby.

Then one of the men starts to get out of the van, making gestures for the child to step in and go with them. You can hear him say something like, "It's alright. Your mom told us to come and pick you up. We can call her on the way to your house."

The child, looking even more distressed than before, isn't sure what to do or what to believe. Something is definitely wrong with this picture. You realize the child is about to be abducted.

What would you do?

Would you run right over there and intervene in any way possible? Would you stand there and watch as a group of strangers take that child away?

I *know* what you would do. You would do exactly what I would do. You would run right over and stop whatever was about to happen. You would protect the child and take him or her away from the danger. I'm sure you'd also write down the van's license plate!

Now imagine that *you* were that child and that you were watching this scene unfold from your adult perspective 20 feet away. You were watching that smaller version of yourself about to be taken. Your instincts would kick in and you would take action to protect that child.

This is how you gain the strength and confidence to honor your boundaries. When you feel your boundaries being crossed, imagine this scenario unfolding and do whatever you can to make sure those people don't accomplish their mission. Look at honoring your boundaries the same way as you would look at protecting the child that you are inside, and you will have the strength, courage, and motivation to do so, regardless of the consequences.

Thinking about consequences is usually what stops you from honoring yourself. There are always going to be consequences for everything you do, but when you honor your boundaries, the consequences of doing so are always justified. When you feel violated, you need to honor yourself and stop the violation by any means necessary. Even if that means others won't be happy with you.

GETTING WHAT YOU REALLY WANT IN LIFE

There is a way to get the *right* relationships, the *right* job, and the results you want almost every time just by asking yourself one question over and over again: Is this right for me?

That's it. That's the magic question you need to ask yourself in almost every moment of your life. The answer will come right away, many times in the form of a feeling, and you'll know if you are on a path that will serve you. Want to test this concept?

Think about a decision you're facing now, or will have to face in the future. Got one? If you can't think of any, make one up!

For example, "Should I move?" "Should I take that job?" "Should I keep reading this book?"

Think of anything that involves a specific decision.

Now that you have the decision in mind, pretend someone is standing in front of you waiting for you to make the choice. They're waiting and there's no more time to contemplate. You need to come up with an answer, right or wrong, in this very moment.

What is your decision? *Make it now.*

What's the feeling coming up for you? You may or may not be able to identify it, but just feel it if it's there. Now ask yourself the question, "Is this decision right for me?" And notice the feeling you get from asking that question. Is it a positive, supportive feeling, or a negative, opposing one? I'll let you decide which feeling is right.

Some people might call this instinct. I call it *intrinsic knowledge*: what you already know at the deepest, subconscious level.

This knowledge resides in a part of your mind you don't think about— your subconscious. It is the part of you that does a lot of processing without your having to lift a finger. It's where your truth resides, and it will steer you right almost every time, even when you think it's wrong. It's how the body communicates with the mind to signal to you which course of action is best.

The mind-body connection is one of the keys to making the right decisions for you. And if you have any doubt about a connection between your physiology and psychology (body and mind), think of something that makes you angry and notice where you *feel* it.

Think of someone who wronged you and hone in on that feeling somewhere in your body. Emotions create feelings inside the body to let you know there's something to be aware of. When you become aware of those feelings, you begin to understand how your subconscious mind with its intrinsic knowledge makes you aware of what's right for you and what's not.

When you made your choice above, what did you feel? Did you feel anything at all? If not, it's possible that you are very good at disconnecting from your emotions, which would certainly skew your results (and give you nothing to work with). Or, if you felt nervous, fearful, or something similar, you might need to start with smaller, easier questions just to learn what "right" feels like for you before tackling the bigger questions in life.

Make Decisions Assertively

No matter where you are with this process, there's one thing you can do to strengthen your accuracy in decisions. It won't be popular, but I guarantee it will start creating new connections at the subconscious level if you're not used to doing this. When you're faced with any decision and you're not sure what choice to make, do this: Make the decision assertively, even if you could be wrong.

This is a scary prospect because it means that A) You could be wrong, and B) You could be judged for being wrong. But what this does inside of you is create very strong references to right and wrong, and build your intrinsic knowledge center so that you are more capable next time. Make decisions like this often enough, and you'll be a superior decision-maker. And soon, you'll be more accurate in your ability to discern between a good decision and a bad one, which is key.

I realize you can't do this if you work in a nuclear power plant or if you are performing open heart surgery. This process needs to be practiced with care, of course. Making decisions assertively, even though you could be wrong, should be done with the less significant decisions in your life. But for most of life's mundane, everyday choices, this is an excellent practice.

This process will also build confidence and wisdom at the same time because it's a fast path to failure or success *every time*. There is no waiting to see what happens as you just test the waters with every step. With every decision you make assertively, you will learn the results fast. Not only that, you'll find that other people tend to gravitate toward people that make decisions confidently.

Attracting others may not be your intention, but it can be a decent side effect if you appreciate a leadership role of any sort. The whole point of making a decision even at the risk of being wrong is to strengthen the connection you have with your subconscious mind, where your deepest knowledge lies. When you're always making safe decisions, you are staying comfortable and never really getting to a deep place in yourself. By staying on the surface, you rarely connect with that intrinsic knowledge. This is why many people, like myself, have felt for most of their lives they've never had any "instincts."

I never felt like I had instinct or that I could trust what I thought was instinct. As time went on, however, and I made decisions that scared me because I wasn't sure if they were right or wrong, I learned more about myself and the paths I should truly follow in life. Even to the point of quitting a job I hated when my wife and I had no money and no place to live.

I asked myself the question, "Is staying at this job right for me?" And the answer was a clear "No!" Then my conscious mind came in and said, "That's nuts! You can't quit! You have no choice but to stay, it's your only income!"

Those words "no choice" were painful. And they felt *wrong* to me. I couldn't get on board with "no choice," so I quit that job knowing that we'd be at the soup kitchen in a week. We were poor at the time, and that job was the only thing keeping us from being dead broke.

Logically, quitting was a bad decision. Looking at all the data, it only made sense to keep working. After all, the alternative was even less desirable. But it wasn't right—I felt it! So I had a hard decision to make, consciously knowing that quitting was a "mistake" but trusting my intrinsic knowledge, my emotional voice, that what I was doing was right.

I did quit, and my wife and I did end up at the soup kitchen. But I was happier than I'd been in a long time. I was no longer bound to a job I hated and the decision to leave a sure thing was exactly what I needed to do. After a few weeks, I confirmed that quitting was the right decision because I eventually found another job that paid double what I was making and also allowed me to travel. I know this sounds a bit esoteric or spiritual, but I don't see it that way. I see it as having been aware enough to make decisions that were right for me, which opened opportunities that wouldn't have been there otherwise.

If I had not quit, I would have gone against what I held to be true for me, and I would also not have been available for the other work that came my way. I would have been happy being unhappy, "knowing" I had no other choice but to stay and tolerate something I loathed.

Making decisions even at the expense of being wrong may not be pleasant at first, but what builds inside you because of it is a lifetime of wisdom and inner trust in yourself. This chapter is dedicated to getting the results you want in life. And a major part of that is to honor your boundaries so that you are showing up in the world as the person you *are*, not the one you believe the world wants to see. Sometimes that means doing things that aren't socially acceptable or "in the norm."

Making decisions assertively, combined with self-compassion, is a powerful way to honor your boundaries and maintain a healthy emotional state. When you approach the world this way, you can give from a more enriched, authentic place. And learning to experience the feeling of right and wrong by trusting your subconscious mind will lead to getting the things you really want in life.

All of these components are part of a larger whole of honoring yourself completely. Being honest with your wants and needs and following through in a way that's congruent inside of you leads to a more fulfilling and rewarding life. And the people who love and support you will do so even more because they will want to be around the more authentic you.

Those who can't support your honoring yourself may not know how to behave around you now that they cannot feed off of your former dysfunctions. They will likely fall away and not be heard from too often. They are the ones that depended on you staying who you were so that they could get *their* needs met. This type of relationship can work but cannot sustain itself for very long.

Sometimes people want you to stay as you are so that you won't grow beyond their comfort level and then leave them behind. This is sad. These people don't want to change and they don't want you to either. They want you to stay at your current level of emotional imbalance so they have someone with whom to empathize (or commiserate).

When you learn to honor yourself, you find out soon enough who honors your honoring yourself, and who would rather you stay where you are so that *they* don't have to change. Honoring your personal boundaries is a huge step along the journey of overcoming your overwhelmed brain. Not having to worry about saying no when you feel like saying no takes a lot of pressure and stress off of you.

Why can't we do that all the time? Why wouldn't we always just say what we mean in every situation? Where does the fear of doing and saying what we honestly want in life come from? Let's talk about that next.

CHAPTER 4

The Path to Healing the Past

MY TRAUMA STORY

I'll never forget the day my stepfather showed up at my mom's house unannounced. I answered the door and was shocked to see the man that I once feared, loved, hated, then moved far away from, standing there asking if he could come in.

He'd left my mom several months previously and I'd never seen her happier since. In fact, I got to know my mom in an entirely new way without his influence in her life. She was finally free of that codependent, abusive relationship, and in my view, every minute of her life was now more fulfilling than it had been for the 44 years she was with him. His alcoholism was one of the primary causes of our family's dysfunction during my childhood.

When you grow up in fear, you develop unique, unhealthy beliefs about the world—many of which are true in your immediate reality but not necessarily true about the world at large. You also develop behaviors to help you survive because day to day, you believe you could be hurt or even killed.

I remember my younger sister and I closing our bedroom doors on many nights, hoping my stepfather (her father) wouldn't come up the stairs in a drunken rage. Some nights he wouldn't stop yelling at our mom for what seemed like hours. As terrifying as this felt, it was also somewhat comforting. After all, if he was yelling, at least we could tell where he was in the house. We could tune into his location just by the sound of his voice. We became very observant and highly sensitive to any sound in the house so that we would always know where he was. We knew that as long as he wasn't at the top of the stairs, we were safe.

One of the more traumatic events happened to me was when I was around five years old. He found stains in my underwear, and that angered him greatly. So he grabbed me, locked my arms under his legs, and held me down on the floor so I couldn't move. He then took my soiled underwear and rubbed them in my face, telling me that "only babies poop their pants!" I was completely immobile and had to endure it until he stopped.

What was worse than his behavior at that moment was the unfortunate fact that I actually believed what he said. I *believed* I was no good and worthless. I accepted that he was right, that I was no longer a baby, and that I should accept my punishment. That event had a dramatic impact in my life and caused me to do more of the very thing he was punishing me about in the first place. For the next few years of childhood, I "pooped" my pants often. I didn't know it then, but I can look back now and realize that my inability to keep my underwear clean as a child was directly related to that one abusive incident and the chain of events that followed. It took me a couple of decades to understand that I had even been abused. I remembered the event clearly, but I didn't think it left any permanent scars. After all, I didn't get "beat up." But because of my dismissive attitude about it, I didn't heal from it for many years.

It took me a long time to discover just how much damage my stepfather had done in those few minutes, let alone for the next 13 years living with him. I believed I was "bad" and "wrong" for the longest time, so getting to a place of realizing I was neither of those things was a life-changing moment and a big improvement over how I *used* to feel about myself.

> **No one should feel guilty about anything they did**
> **or didn't do when they were five years old.**

A couple of years after that particular episode, I stopped going to the bathroom altogether, so my mom had to take me to the hospital. They gave her a formula of mineral oil and fruit juice to feed me every day. They also gave her something else, something that created one of the biggest phobias of my life: a suppository.

Of everything that I feared happening to me in my childhood, getting an enema was one of the most horrifying experiences of my life. I was so traumatized by that one incident that I became highly sensitive and even developed a phobia that I carried with me well into my forties. I was afraid of anyone going near my butt for any reason, and I would cringe every time someone mentioned that area of the body.

I was only able to recover from that *just a few months ago,* as of this writing. It was one of the final, major hurdles of healing I had to go through to release the remaining trauma from that time in my life. It was also the hardest step of my entire journey. When you're emotionally abused, it's hard to pinpoint exactly what someone did to you to cause you to be in a dysfunctional space today. However, when there's any type of *physical* trauma or abuse, the effects are typically more clear, and there are often many more sensitivities that develop.

Physical abuse is hard on the spirit because it's not just the mental memory of what happened—the body remembers it too. Emotional scars are more or less invisible to the world, so few people can really tell what happened to you. However, when you're physically abused, it can create some real havoc in your life. Think of the dog that gets hit or slapped if it pees on the floor. He will become more fearful and sensitive over time, to the point he'll cower and hide if he sees anyone raise their hand for any reason. We remember physical abuse and how we felt at the time, so we respond in a physical way as if it were happening again, *even if we have no conscious memory of the abuse.*

Your Body Knows

There are times when *only* the body remembers an event from the past (called a kinesthetic memory) because the mind has a self-protection mechanism in place that allows it to "check out" and disconnect from the physical senses. I've seen this with cases of sexual abuse and other traumas where the situation was just too painful or overwhelming to deal with. This "checking out" is called dissociation, and it can work really well in the moment because it helps a person, especially a child who often has no choice in the matter, to disconnect from the physical or psychological pain that can accompany a traumatic experience.

When you have no actual auditory or visual memory of a trauma but are still carrying around anguish of some sort, you may not even know what you need to heal from.

When something triggers us, just like an abused dog afraid of someone's hand, the body can relive the original abuse. It doesn't usually bring back the original pain, but it can create a similar physical response. This is what I mean when I say the body remembers. For example, if you were kicked in the stomach as a kid and today you interpreted someone's movement as a kick, you might immediately block your stomach and turn. Though this could be a way to protect yourself just in case it ever happens again, the ideal situation, of course, is to not be with people that might do that to you in the first place.

The body is a great signaling machine. Have you ever thought of why we open our mouths when we're surprised, or why we put our hands on our face when we say, "Oh no!"? There are reasons behind all of our physical gestures but most people don't think twice about it. For example, you might cover your mouth if you're surprised. If so, deep down you may have a primal instinct to keep quiet so you're not heard. Whether that developed as a protection mechanism when you were younger or it's hardwired into your DNA, it's the perfect example of how the body responds when it gets triggered.

RELEASING EMOTIONAL BAGGAGE

Emotional Freedom Technique

I was fully present when I got an enema at seven years old, so I remember the event quite well. I healed emotionally but the physical memory stuck with me all my life as a kinesthetic, phobic reaction. That is until I addressed it in an unconventional way, using something I believed to be a bit "hokey," called EFT, or Emotional Freedom Technique. If you look it up, you'll see people tapping their body and saying what appear to be affirmations.

If you've ever listened to *The Overwhelmed Brain* podcast, you already know I'm not a big fan of affirmations because they often feel like you're lying to yourself. However, the way they are utilized in EFT seems to cause a neutralization effect between what's good for you and something you don't want. For example, self-love and self-compassion are good for you because they help you to take care of yourself. But fear of something like swimming might be something you don't want, so perhaps eliminating that fear would be beneficial in your life.

With EFT, you begin the process with a setup phrase, and it can feel really corny when you say it. But I think the fact that it can feel a little uncomfortable and strange at the same time is part of what makes it work. It's just something you wouldn't normally say when you're going through a challenge. For example, using the fear of swimming, your setup phrase might be something like, "Even though I'm afraid of swimming, I deeply and completely love myself."

If you've never done EFT, this probably sounds weird. But experiencing the feeling of not wanting to say it appears to be an important part of the emotional release process. I have other theories on why EFT can work (including the possibility that it might be doing what's called a "pattern interrupt"), but I won't be diving into them in this book. I wanted to mention Emotional Freedom Technique, however, because it is exactly what helped me get over a 36-year phobia in a matter of 15 minutes!

Right now, I no longer cringe when anyone mentions that previously taboo area of my body. I might still have a little more work to do, but I feel confident enough now where I could actually get a physical examination from a doctor without too much fear. That's phenomenal, considering the very thought of visiting a doctor used to paralyze me.

Emotional Freedom Technique may or may not work for you, but it's worth looking into if you're dealing with anything that you just can't seem to get rid of. Almost all of the information you need is online and free, so I encourage you to check it out, though I've provided a quick step by step below (please note my steps are highly condensed). And even though it worked for me, I still think it's a little hokey. But perhaps feeling ridiculous while you tap your body is one of the reasons it *does* work, strange as that seems.

The Technique

1. Think of anything that you'd like to feel better about—something that bothers you now that you wish didn't. We'll call that "The Problem."

2. Rate The Problem from 1 to 10, 1 being no negative feelings or pain whatsoever and 10 being the worst pain imaginable.

3. Say the following: "Even though I _____, I deeply and completely accept myself." Fill in the blank with The Problem (e.g., "Even though I [have this sore back] or [can't stop thinking about my ex] or [am afraid of spiders], I deeply and completely accept myself."). Say this three times, even if it feels silly.

4. Now comes the tapping part. Tap on the following areas of your body around seven to 10 times per area, each time repeating The Problem. For example, as you tap on an area, say "my sore back," "thinking about my ex," "spiders," or whatever it is for you.

Where to tap:

  a. The top of your head

  b. Next to either eyebrow (on the inside of the brow)

  c. Right under your eye

  d. Right under your nose

  e. Right under your lips

  f. Your collarbone

  g. Four inches below your armpit

5. Repeat step 4 two more times.

6. Take a deep breath.

Repeat steps 2 through 6 two more times, each time noticing if your original rating from step 2 changes at all.

After three complete rounds, notice if anything else comes up during your tapping. If other problems arise, you can tap on those too.

This exercise is a very basic version of the Emotional Freedom Technique. You might have found that it completely resolved an issue you were having, or did nothing at all. I have not found this to work for everything, but when it works, it works really well. Again, search online for more information if you want to look into this further. There are many videos that show the process in action.

░░

Physical Trigger Points

If you've experienced any type of abuse or trauma where you were dissociated, or disconnected from your auditory and/or visual senses, you might find yourself now reacting when touched on certain areas of your body or in a particular way.

I remember massaging my girlfriend's feet one night. It was a nice moment and she was enjoying the attention. But I must have rubbed a point on her body that triggered a kinesthetic memory of some sort because she almost immediately went into what a therapist might call a "full regression," where she acted as if she were reexperiencing a trauma from her past. She started off crying, but soon she experienced almost uncontrollable movement of all her limbs. She looked as if she was being held down against her will. Had anyone else been watching, they might have thought she was possessed.

Fortunately, because I knew of the abuse in her past, I quickly figured out that I triggered a memory of one of her abusive episodes. It was entirely unpleasant to watch, but more so for her to go through. However, while she was going through it, I let her know that she was safe *here and now* and that it would soon pass. I wanted to remind her that I was there for her and that no matter what, she was going to be fine. And within a few minutes, it did pass.

After it was over, we talked about it. She was grateful I didn't run out of the room screaming. We both knew, given our own backgrounds and our work with abuse survivors, what had happened to her. Whatever abuse or trauma she went through as a child was being replayed in that very moment.

The body can and does respond from repressed emotions through physical trigger points. What triggered her that night was my touching a specific area of her leg, which sent her into orbit, for lack of a better term. The trigger did not spark an auditory or visual memory of that past event, but the physical recurrence of it was very real. She even said it felt as if she were a child that was being forced to do something against her will.

Since she and I have been together, this type of full-body, physical regression has happened twice. A few days after both instances, she experienced a huge release of emotional baggage that she didn't even realize she was carrying. She told me it was because she has never been with anyone that made her feel safe like I did, which is extremely important when it comes to releasing any emotions that you are holding on to from the past.

Finding someone safe with whom to share and express yourself is one of the keys to emotional release of any kind. You don't always have that option and you *can* do it on your own, but having a person in your life that you trust makes the process go a bit faster. When it comes to emotional baggage, the safer you feel, the more likely you'll be able to release it.

THE PERMISSION TO BE VULNERABLE

Having what I call a "safe zone" to express yourself is so important to healing and growing from past trauma. You have to feel safe in the environment and the person you're with. If those two factors don't exist, it's a lot harder to release the negative emotions you might be carrying around. Just having that safe place to verbalize what's happening inside you can be all you need to release many years of repressed fear, hurt, or anger.

The typical challenge is finding someone who will let you express yourself without giving you their opinion or judging what you say. When you find someone like that, you'll feel comfortable and protected knowing that anything you do or say is okay and that you won't be looked down upon or made to feel bad about what you're expressing.

That's a great reason to a have a good friend. Or at least someone you feel safe with, whether it's a therapist, counselor, or coach like myself. It's important that you trust the person you're with so that you can express things you feel embarrassed about or ashamed of, hold guilt about, or anything else that's going on inside of you, because holding on to this stuff only makes it worse. And it wears you down over time.

> **Life is a lot less enjoyable when you hold on
> to what doesn't serve you any longer.**

I had a female client that found it very hard to express herself because she never felt safe. She wanted to express her true thoughts and feelings but never felt she could trust anyone enough to be that vulnerable. After talking with her a while, I came to learn that her roommate was the safest person she's ever known. She never felt threatened by him and had always felt like she could share anything with him. He was also gay, so that was a bonus because there was little chance for attraction and romantic emotions that might get in the way.

It was the ideal scenario. She had been holding on to some heavy emotional baggage, and for the first time, she realized that she might be able to actually express and release some of it to the person she was living with. She had simply never considered sharing things with him before because she thought her painful past was hers alone to bear. I asked her to take a leap of faith and share things with him that she's never shared with anyone, including incidents that made her feel ashamed or embarrassed.

She was nervous about doing it but excited at the same time. What she didn't know was that by not sharing, she was holding on to the very thing that was sabotaging her happiness. It may sound melodramatic, but this can be the absolute truth of what happens in your life when you don't release unresolved negative emotions.

> **The longer you hold on and choose not to express your emotional pain, the longer misery will plague your life.**

This is a vital truth to etch into your brain because there's so much pain that isn't released over the years. We carry with us all of these open loops, which keep us searching for peace and freedom, but we never find it. I use the term "open loop" to indicate some sort of unfinished business in your mind, like the cliffhanger at the end of a movie or TV show. You know there's more to come, so the story lingers in your mind until you see the conclusion, closing the loop.

If you ever get angry with someone and feel like screaming at them but choose not to, you could create an open loop so that you hold on to that anger as if someday you'll choose to express it to them. The anger gets into that open state, then you carry it around with you! And every time you see the person that made you angry, you get emotionally triggered and you don't want to be near them.

It's possible that by finally yelling at them and telling them what's been on your mind, you'd close the loop and let go of the anger. This would give you that conclusion to that unfinished business you were seeking, and you might get to have peace with that subject again. Or at least, you'd be able to let go of a lot of the anger around it. Expressing yourself in this way could essentially help you to release your grip on the anger or any other negative emotions that can cause so much stress in your mind and body.

It reminds me of a video game from the eighties called Warlords. In the game, you must defend your castle against a flying dragon that spits fireballs at you. You play against other players who are also defending their castles. When a fireball comes your way, you can either reflect it by bouncing it off your shield or you can catch it, giving you the opportunity to aim the fireball at an opponent's castle with accuracy. Catching and holding on to the fireball gives you a better chance of success because you can make your shot count. The drawback to that, however, is that as you hold on to it, the fire will drip back onto your own castle walls, eating away at it brick by brick.

This is what I equate to holding on to emotional pain from the past. The longer you hold on to it, the more your emotional foundation is slowly chipped away until you release it. Once you are able to fully let go of emotional pain, it no longer poses a threat to your emotional health.

It's an illusion to believe there's any advantage to holding on to emotional pain. It burns away at your personal foundation over time. It sticks around as an underlying, continuous unpleasantness simmering in the depths of your psyche. And often the only way you know that it exists is because you feel something is missing in your life. You feel that there must be more to living than "this." You may even feel like a victim who has a lot of bad luck and just can't catch a break.

It's like that movie line, "Is this as good as it gets?" Holding on to emotional pain makes you feel like you should be happier and not be so down all the time. Almost always, when you can't figure out why you're not feeling better than you are, you can point to some emotional pain you're holding on to. Of course, having a physical illness or condition can also create emotional pain. You can be angry *about* a physical illness or condition, which actually makes you feel worse than you already feel. This is why it's so important to find that safe zone I mentioned earlier so that you can be the truest version of yourself without fear of judgment.

You need to be okay being vulnerable, and that can be hard to accomplish when you don't feel safe. The vulnerable part of you holds on to your pain, anger, and fear, and connecting with that part of yourself is the path to releasing those very same things. As soon as you are able to connect with some of your deep-rooted emotions, you start the process of releasing them. Sometimes just identifying your most painful emotions allows them to rise to the surface to be processed or released. The challenge with the process is knowing that you might wind up reliving pain in order to release it. That doesn't mean you *have* to relive it, as there are other ways to release emotional pain. But if you can accept that you might experience *some* unpleasant emotions and that they will only last for a short period of time, you will create a path for those emotions to rise up and out of you.

Acceptance of emotional pain helps release emotional pain.

Acceptance helps you flow through challenges. It is the opposite of resistance, which causes you to suffer through challenges. When you are unable to accept something in your life, you create a resistance to it, causing it to feel worse than it is. Most people don't want to accept that they have to re-experience emotional pain in order to release it. They would rather believe that it will decrease over time on its own and never get any more painful than it is. But when they hold on to anger, fear, or upset in any way, they end up prolonging their misery so that the pain never decreases. It becomes less prevalent but not less intense, and it can be triggered at any moment.

Release Negative Emotions

If you have any negative emotions that you've been unable to release but would like to, here are a few questions to help you get the process started. Don't worry, I won't make you drudge up anything awful. The questions are worded in a way to help you explore your attachment to any painful thoughts or emotions you may have lingering inside of you.

1. Do you really want to release these emotions?

Does anything besides *yes* come up for you? Quite often, you might find a reason to keep the emotions you don't want, strange as that sounds. That's because you might see a benefit to keeping them. For example, by keeping the anger about your uncle, you believe it shows him that you are not weak and will never let him get to you again. You may not like the feeling of being angry, but you keep the anger as a protection against him.

What seems to be a way of protecting yourself turns out to be harmful, because the anger stays in you and eats away at you day after day. What's really happening is that you are hurting *yourself* more than anything. You're holding on to that proverbial fireball as the flame spits back onto your foundation, burning away at it brick by brick.

2. Do you know how to feel anything else?

This may seem like a silly question at first, but think about how long you've held on to the negative emotions. Do you remember a time you didn't feel that way? Was it a long time ago? Sometimes it's hard to remember what it felt like before the bad emotions stepped in and took over. When you've been carrying them around for so long, it feels almost normal.

3. What would you like to feel instead?

It's helpful to know what you'd rather feel so that you have some sort of direction to go in. If your answer is "I just want to be happy," then break it down a little bit. Figure out *what* would make you happy. What needs to change in order for you to be happy?

Be realistic too. If you want to say something like, "I just want my uncle to get out of my life forever," then you will have a hard time getting what you want because you are hoping something happens that is outside of your control. Which leads to the next question.

4. If you could do anything you wanted without a fear of the consequences, what would you do?

This is a great question to ask yourself because it takes away fear, doubt, and hesitation. If you could do *anything* and there were no negative consequences for your behavior, what would you do?

|||||||||||||||||||||||||||||||||||||||||||||||||||||||||||||||||||||||||||||||||||||||||||||||||||||||||||||||

When it comes to repressed, negative emotions, one way to resolve them is to take action on them. Using the uncle example again, that might mean calling him up and telling him how wrong and bad he is for everything he's ever done to you. Doing that could actually make you feel a lot better, as all of that previously unexpressed emotion would be expressed and might be a huge release for you.

The challenge with that, however, is that it's not always safe to express yourself in such a way, nor do you always have the courage to follow through. There might be something holding you back. Maybe you don't want to create a family drama or open up any further dialog that will only lead to more hostility, or something else. There are a multitude of reasons you might not want to confront people head on.

Full and honest expression of self is what I teach, but sometimes you simply aren't prepared to do so. You have to go through a build-up process before you get to a point where you can honor your boundaries in the moment.

Standing up for yourself places a lot of bricks into your emotional foundation, though you may not always be prepared for the consequences of doing so.

EMPOWERMENT COMES FROM HONORING YOURSELF

"Power" is empowerment. It is where you want to be with every decision in your life. It's what gives you the strength to make the tough choices for yourself and others, and it also allows you to express yourself in the moment instead of suppress how you feel indefinitely. *Full* empowerment is taking full control of your life by showing others where your boundaries are and not letting them walk on you. When you feel full empowerment, you walk confidently knowing you can handle almost anything that comes your way.

Getting to that point is a process, and it can take some time to develop that process because you may not have been taught that it's okay to be expressive and honor yourself. The toughest part about empowerment, however, can be the realization that honoring yourself may cost you some relationships. And that's a tough pill to swallow. When you want to honor yourself and express your truth, you may lose people you'd rather not lose from your life.

In most of my previous relationships, I chose not to honor what I really wanted and did my best to make sure my partner was happy all the time, even at the cost of my own happiness. I believed it was better to honor my partner, even when they weren't honoring me.

Remember what I said earlier: Honoring others over yourself is like dishonoring yourself.

I dishonored myself for many years. Not only in my relationships, but also in my friendships and with family. I would honor other people who were not honoring me. There's no sense to that, because what's the point of honoring others if it leads to your unhappiness? What's the point of being in relationships where others are allowed to be happy but you are not?

You are absolutely allowed to be happy, so honor yourself in a way you want others to honor you. That means if someone is being disrespectful, you might have to speak up and let them know. And if they don't know how to be any other way, or choose not to treat you any differently, then maybe they are not the type of person you need to be around.

Author and motivational speaker Jim Rohn said, "You are the average of the five people you spend the most time with." Who do you spend the most time with? Are those the people you want to be more like? Do you look up to them? Do they care about you and support you?

These are all very important questions, because your level of happiness is sometimes directly related to the quality of the people around you. That may sound like the opposite of New Age thinking, where "you can be happy inside yourself and the world will be a better place because of it," but it's hard to stay in a happy state when there are negative influences in your environment. Sometimes you need to let go of negative people, even when you have a lot of time, energy, and love invested in them.

**Sometimes the hardest decision to make in
life is the one that best serves you.**

If you had no toxic people in your life, what would that be like? Really think about it... what would life be like at work or home? What would it be like to spend time on your own or with others that only want the best for you?

The good news is as you change inside, toxic people start disappearing from your life. Since toxic people feed off of dysfunction, the more dysfunctional behavior inside you, the more they have to feed off of.

Toxic people thrive around dysfunctional people, and they will stay in your life indefinitely as long as you still have healing to do within. Once you've grown and healed, however, you're going to be making healthier decisions for yourself. Those decisions include who you choose to keep in your life and who you choose to be away from. And soon, who's leftover are only those that support you being the best you possible.

YOUR INNER CHILD'S PERSPECTIVE

When I answered the door to my mom's house and saw my stepfather standing there, I cringed on the inside. I never thought I'd have to deal with him again. But the universe has a funny way of presenting you with challenges to test what you've learned about yourself.

I really believed that I had come to a place of honoring my boundaries and that no matter what happened, I could easily stand up for myself and those I loved without hesitation. The man I once loved and feared, then hated, then loved again, then released from my life forever, showed up, almost as if to say, "Here I am, the same as always; who are you going to be?"

That really is a great question. When you've been through some healing and growth in yourself, will you show up as the new you or the one people have always known you to be? In families, this is an especially important question, because family typically has the same perspective of us our entire life. So sometimes if we try to show up in a different way, we might end up reverting back to our old selves because we find out that we just can't communicate with them from this new version of us.

Imagine you hadn't seen your father in a year and every time you connected with him prior to that, you ended up leaving the conversation angry. Now that a year has passed, however, you've had time to heal some old emotional wounds and do some personal growth. Do you think next time you meet up with him you'd still get angry, at least in the same way that you did before? How do you think your communication would change if you processed and released some of your own stuff over the year?

Your communication would certainly change, because *behavior feeds off of behavior*. Your reactions feed other people's responses. And if your reactions change, their responses will change. It's like what I said before: "Toxic people feed off your dysfunction."

When you react the way you've reacted in the past, you'll get the same dysfunctional responses. When my stepfather arrived at my mom's door months after he left her, I immediately felt fear rush through me. In fact, I felt a wave of several thoughts and emotions because not only was I surprised to see him, but now I had to come to a place inside me where I was to either submit to his insistence of letting him in (something my mom did not want) or stand my ground and have a confrontation with him for the first time in my life.

I have never stood up to my stepfather. Yet there I was, face to face with him, knowing I had a choice to make. The fear of what might happen mixed with the years of personal growth and healing I'd done came to a head. What I chose at that moment was going to define me and our relationship from that point forward.

I knew that if I acquiesced and let him in, all those years of becoming the man I believed myself to be would have been lost. I realize that sounds somewhat dramatic, but it's moments like this that shape how we feel about ourselves and how we are treated by others going forward. To *not* let him in, or even prevent him from coming in, would be a leap into the unknown, a clear defiance, which is something I'd always feared doing with him. All of these thoughts were going through my head in nanoseconds, but the choice had to be made.

Finally, I made my decision based on one philosophy that I promised I would always follow, which is to honor myself without fear of the consequences. As I stood in the doorway facing my stepfather, I let go of my fear of the consequences and told him that he couldn't come in. I said, "Sorry, you can't come in. And Mom doesn't want you here anyway."

It was the hardest thing I've ever said to anyone in my life.

Making decisions based on what's right for you is empowering. Making them because of fear of the consequences is giving your power away.

After I spoke those words, I waited for the shove...or the punch... or the yelling...but none of that happened. The fear of what might happen next finally did rise up in me after that, but what I believed might happen never did. I was standing there truly waiting to for a fist to come flying at me, or worse.

Instead, he shrugged his shoulders and said, "Okay," then walked away.

I couldn't believe what had just happened. Not only did I pass the ultimate test in my own personal growth, but I also prevented a very bad situation from occurring. If I had let him in because of my fear (what I always felt around him every other time in my life), then a bad situation could have certainly developed. He was a very toxic person and letting him back in at that moment would have set me back many years and put my mom in harm's way.

I chose a path of honoring myself without fear. I decided not to play out any scenario in my head of what *might* happen if I said one thing or another. I just searched within to figure out what the right decision was. In the moments of your life where you have a choice to honor yourself or those your love, focus on what's right, not what you fear. This small shift is what it takes to honor yourself at the most challenging times. Ask yourself what the right decision is and don't play out a scenario of what might happen *after* you make that decision, just make the decision.

IIII **EXERCISE** IIIIIIIIIIIIIIIIIIIIIIIIIIIIIIIIIIIIIIIIIIIIIIIIIIIIIIIIIIIIIIIIIIIIIIIIIIIIIIIIIIIIIIIIIIIIIIIIIIIIIIIIIII

Make the Decision That's Right for You

Think about a time in the past when you had to face someone that was very unpleasant, and you had to make a choice to either honor yourself or honor their dishonoring you. If you chose to honor them over yourself, that's the kind of scenario I want you to work with.

Do you have that unpleasant person or situation in mind? The following questions will help you determine if at that time, you made a choice that empowered you or one that took that power away. These questions are worded as if this situation has already happened, so if you're thinking about something in the future, you'll need to improvise a little bit. Don't write down your answers, just think about each question as you go through the list and be open to any thought that comes up for you.

1. When you think about the decision you made, does it make you feel good?

2. After you made that decision, did your life get easier, harder, or stay the same?

3. Knowing what you know now, if you could go back and make a different decision, would you?

4. Was your decision based on fear of what might happen, or what you felt was right for you in the moment?

5. If you knew there would be no consequences to any decision you made, would you have made a different one?

6. How would things be different for you if you made a different decision at that time?

You can do this exercise for any number of decisions you've made. What you end up with is *reflection*. When you reflect upon the decisions that you've faced in your life, you reexamine them from a different perspective. Reflection is easy to do when you're alone in your thoughts, but when someone asks you specific questions regarding those events, you get a chance to revisit the events from a difference perspective. This helps you understand where you were at the time and why you made the choices you made.

A Decision Based on Fear

I can think of few kids I knew in high school that I prefer to never see again. One in particular chose to rip apart the shirt I wore to school one day until it was a tattered mess. His friends cheered him on and laughed while I tried to save what was left of my shirt. I went the rest of the day with barely a shirt and a lot of humiliation.

When I think back to that moment, I remember I had a choice. I could either stop his behavior (honor myself) or allow his behavior (honor him). The choice I made defined my relationship with him, my relationship to those watching, and my relationship to myself from that point on. As you might guess, when you have a choice like this to make, what you decide can set in motion what could be "the way it is" for the rest of your life. If you're thinking, "Wow, it sounds like making the wrong choice could have a big impact on me," you're right.

It doesn't mean you'll always know the right path to take, but it does help you consider what might happen if you choose one path over another. The challenge is knowing the right path for you.

When I think about where I was when that high school bully was ripping my shirt, I remember making the decision to laugh instead of standing up and honoring myself. I figured he would have no reason to continue if he realized I wasn't embarrassed. But that didn't stop him. He kept at it until he was satisfied. I made my decision based on fear of being hurt instead of what I believed to be right for me.

That one decision also reinforced my already prevalent feelings of low self-worth and kept me as the target of many jokes for the next few years. When I do the exercise on page 66, I think the most important question that comes to my mind is, "How would things have changed had I made a different decision?" The answer that comes up makes me feel strong and confident. I think back to that moment and realize that if I had stood up for myself and stopped his behavior, I would have been viewed differently by everyone. I would no longer be seen as a pushover and people would have stopped taking advantage of me. In fact, I would have carried that with me into every relationship and career as I grew older.

One decision like that can change your life. It's quite possible I could have gotten into a fight had I forcibly stopped him, but now that I know what I know, I would have accepted that as a consequence. And I am definitely not one to pick a fight. I try to avoid them at all costs! But the difference is that I would no longer focus on my fear of getting hurt (which can certainly happen). I'd focus on what I need to do in the moment and deal with the consequences later. That doesn't mean I'd walk through a shady neighborhood at night carrying a bag of money, but it does mean that if I'm ever faced with the decision to honor myself or honor someone who is dishonoring me, I will consider myself first.

This is a commitment to a philosophy, but not necessarily an absolute. Whenever possible, honor yourself. Make a commitment to that way of life and you'll often get exactly what you want. It can be truly challenging to honor yourself at times, but the reward of doing so far outweighs the rut you go back into when you don't.

The most important point out of all of this is not what will happen when you honor yourself, but what will happen when you *don't*. What happens to your power when you make choices out of fear? You lose it and get stuck in the same patterns over and over again.

If you had no fear of the consequences, what would you do?

IS LIVING A FEARLESS LIFE POSSIBLE?

What if you had no fear? What decision would you make then? The person you become tomorrow is based on the decisions you make today. So when you're face to face with something that involves a hard choice, like the one I had to make when I met my stepfather at my mom's front door, you can make the choice to be the person you've always been or the one you've worked hard to become. If, however, you continue to bring your childhood fears and insecurities into your adult world, you'll continue to respond to the world as if you were still that child.

There will be moments in life that give you a chance to find out who you've really become. With many people, you might have no problem honoring yourself and saying what's on your mind. But the true test will be when you meet someone you share a history with. I shared a long, turbulent history with my stepfather, so old fears came back. I still thought of him as more powerful than me in many ways. But then

I realized that I needed to embrace and honor this new person I've become; otherwise I'd be embracing that old, child's perspective of the world. I was scared of a lot back when I was a kid, and I did not want to be that person again.

I've said it in a few different ways now, but if you're going to take anything away from this book, remember that the true path into your empowerment is to embrace what you need to do for you in the moment and not think ahead too much about what might happen. It can be a leap of faith to honor yourself, but once you're over that hump you will have the confidence to do it again and not be anyone's doormat.

|||| **EXERCISE** |||||||||||||||||||||||||||||||||||||||||||||||||||||||||||||||||||||||||||||||||||||||||||||||

Imagine If You Had No Fear

Think of a decision you might make today if you had no fear of the consequences. Write your answer below:

_____

_____

_____

_____

Your answer doesn't automatically set in stone what you need to do, I just wanted you to consider what you would do if you had no fear. Believe it or not, that exercise in itself is a path to a very powerful resource inside you. Just imagining what it would be like to be without fear puts you into an entirely different state of mind. And as you imagine a scenario, you may even want to think beyond that moment and consider what life would be like a month or even a year from that point. Would it be the same? Would you be the same? Or would things be entirely different?

|||||||||||||||||||||||||||||||||||||||||||||||||||||||||||||||||||||||||||||||||||||||||||||||||||||||||||||||

Having no fear doesn't mean you pick fights with people you know can physically hurt or even kill you—you still have to choose your battles wisely. But it does help you realize what's right for you and those you love. You *know* what's right for you because it fills your veins; you can feel it through your body, and it motivates you to take action. All you have to do is follow that feeling and honor yourself in the moment. Knowing what's right can sometimes even help you override fear.

Look at fear as an attempt to avoid pain. As a child, when you didn't want to feel pain, you made decisions that kept you from that pain. But as an adult, you don't have to fear some of the things you used to. That fear is old. That pain is old. I realize it can still exist inside you and might need healing, but the first step to healing is to start honoring yourself no matter what.

It can be a huge step into unknown territory for sure. I actually believed that my stepfather was going to punch me when I stopped him from coming in. I waited for it! And it didn't happen. But if it did, I still would not have regretted my decision to keep him out of the house. In fact, I would have embraced it even more, knowing that I made the right choice.

Don't let your inner child's perspective of the world rule your life. Start seeing the world from the eyes of the person you are today. Don't get too lost in the "what ifs" because that will cause you to make decisions based on fear. Had I listened to my fear of "What if he kills me?" I wouldn't have passed my test that day and my stepfather might have caused a lot of damage in many ways.

Being in a relationship with someone you fear and loathe, like my mom was with my stepfather for many years, is a self-imposed prison sentence. And it's one many people really believe they have no choice but to serve. My mother kept herself in this prison by being an integral part of a dysfunctional feedback machine. Her generosity and kindness fed into my stepfather's selfishness and abusiveness. And his need for someone to take care of him fed into my mom's belief that if she made him happy, he would treat her better. It was a vicious, repetitive cycle that never ended.

That's how relationships are sometimes. You can be so close to your problem that you can't see it, even when it's right in front of you. Or if you do see it, you believe there's nothing you can do about it because you feel like you have no choice but to stay in a situation you committed to. Remember, you should only keep commitments that continue to serve both of you in a healthy way. The level and quality of your partner is in direct proportion to the level of healing you need to do in yourself. When you look over your past relationships, you can probably see a correlation between where you were in your personal growth and healing and where they were in their level of dysfunction.

The more healed you are within, the more healthy partners you attract and keep. The more healing you need to do, however, is almost always reflected in the type of person you end up with. So if you're looking over at your husband, wife, boyfriend, or girlfriend, and asking yourself how in the world you ended up with that person, remember that who you are is what attracted you to them and them to you in the first place.

Want better relationships? Heal yourself first and foremost, and you will almost always get a partner that has achieved a very similar level of healing and growth themselves. Let's talk about who you attract and what that reveals about you next.

CHAPTER 5

How Relationships Reflect What Needs to Heal in You

The hardest relationships you've been through can be the best learning experiences if you take the lessons from them as opportunities to grow. When you focus more on how bad or wrong your ex was instead of healing from whatever attracted you to that type of person in the first place, you may end up reliving that bad relationship with the same type of partner in the future.

When I met the woman who became my wife, she showed me a list of criteria that her "perfect man" had to meet. She wasn't going to settle for anything less. When I looked at it, I was very surprised that I met nearly every single condition, except maybe one or two. She figured it was close enough, so we started seeing each other.

However, what she didn't have on her list was something that may have prevented years of misery for her. Though I qualified as a "great catch" according to her criteria, I did not meet her relationship values (see Chapter 2). One of her most important values in relationships was to feel safe with the person she was with. I was not a safe person back then.

I was full of judgment and criticism. I believed I knew what was best for her, so I couldn't support her in behavior I disagreed with. I didn't like that she ate junk food, nor how little she exercised. Needless to say, I was very difficult to live with. I set unrealistically high standards that were nearly impossible to meet. And even if she were able to meet them, I'm sure I would have found even more to judge.

That's how judgmental people are—they will always find more to judge or criticize you about. You will never be free of their judging eyes until they change. The problem is they typically don't change unless they experience a radical shift in perspective or they feel threatened by a big loss (someone leaving them, for example). And even if they do change, will it last? Only time will tell if that's possible.

Except for the relationship I'm in now, I've judged every single romantic partner I've ever been with. Some of them had more tolerance than others, so those relationships lasted longer. But every relationship that could have been great, I systematically destroyed through my dysfunctional behavior. That's because I held on to one belief that disintegrated each and every one of them, and I refused to let go of that belief because I "knew" I was right. The loss of love, time and time again, couldn't convince me that I was making bad choices that were based on a faulty belief.

It took me up until about four years ago to figure out that this one belief ruined my life and caused the breakdown of every good relationship I had.

LIMITING BELIEFS

A belief that doesn't serve you and causes you more misery than happiness is called a "limiting belief." I'm not very fond of that term because it is so overused nowadays, but it is a good description for what it does: it limits you.

Limiting beliefs cause you to believe your own thoughts in ways that work against you. It's like believing water is bad for you, so you refuse to drink it. Eventually you will suffer, because without water you cannot survive. Believing something is good that isn't, or believing something is bad that is actually good, are both ways that beliefs can work against you.

The one limiting belief that I carried with me into all of my relationships was this:

When my partner does something I don't like, I need to change them.

This was a belief I *knew* to be true and chose to follow in all of my relationships. It helped destroy much of my satisfaction and happiness in life. I fully believed that "when she changes, I'll be happier".

If my wife stopped eating junk food, which was a huge trigger for me at the time, I believed our lives would be much happier and I wouldn't be upset. I focused all of my time and energy on her changing, thinking I was being helpful. My marriage, finite as it was, turned out to be the most paramount lesson of my life because it was the one that cured me of my judgmental behavior. My ex-wife was very sensitive to my judgments, which caused her a lot of pain and feelings of neglect. Not only did her inability to get beyond her food addiction cause her grief, but my judgments about her addiction caused her to feel even worse about herself. She would then bury the pain through emotional eating. It was a vicious, never-ending cycle of feeling bad, being made to feel worse, and then trying to block pain. Until she left me for good.

My attitude was what drove the wedge between us and hammered in the final nail of our marital coffin. My focus on her changing instead of my healing was what led to its demise altogether. If I had only made another choice, we might still be married today. I'm not saying that decision would necessarily have resulted in the best outcome for either of us, but just knowing that there were other paths I could have taken makes me wonder how things would have been different.

There are always other choices you can make at any time in your life, in any situation. But sometimes you can't see those choices while you're in the thick of things. And if anyone came up to you and said, "The reason you're getting the results you are is because you are choosing the life you are living," you might actually get upset with them.

Suffering happens when you believe you have no choice. It's when you think you're stuck with no way out. But choices do exist, even when you think they don't. It's just that sometimes you don't want to face such choices because making them might mean the end of something you might not want to end. Or it could mean completely uprooting your current life and starting a new one. But staying in a situation where you are suffering in any way is not a way to live. The truth is, you almost always have a choice. Four of them to be exact.

THE FOUR CHOICES

This may be the most controversial section of this book because it forces you to make a choice. The choice you make, once you fully embrace and accept it, will get you through almost any conflict or strife in your relationships and maybe even your life in general.

Most of life's struggles come from *resisting* what is. When you refuse to accept that a particular person or job will never change, you create resistance inside your mind and body. This resistance causes stress and overwhelm because you don't want the thing you resist to be true. Yet, no matter what you do, it *stays* true. In other words, the more you resist a problem, the more that problem persists.

In the same sense, the more you don't like your partner's behavior, the more your partner's behavior will bother you. Furthermore, you'll find yourself blaming them for your unhappiness. Often when you're unhappy in a relationship, all of your time and energy becomes focused on what your partner needs to do to change, and not what you need to do to honor yourself.

You've probably echoed statements similar to these from time to time:

"If she would only stop doing that, we'd be fine."

"If he would only stop talking to me that way, we would be happy again."

Unfortunately, sometimes you only focus on what triggers the problem and not the actual foundation of the problem itself. The problem usually isn't what you think it is. In fact, you may not agree with this, but if you are having any trouble in your relationship because of something your partner is doing, your focus is on the wrong person. When your partner does something you don't like, you are responsible for where the relationship goes from there.

You have a choice.

If you find yourself more unhappy than happy in your relationship, you probably don't realize that you're making choices that feed into that unhappiness. And any choice that feeds into unhappiness is an unhealthy choice. If there are problems in the relationship and you want to take healthier, more productive steps toward happiness, select one of the four choices below.

1. If you can't accept the problem, solve it.

2. If you can't solve the problem, adapt to it.

3. If you can't adapt to the problem, walk away from it.

4. If you can't walk away from the problem, accept it.

Remember I told you that this chapter is going to force you to make a choice? This is where it all happens. And how you choose will determine your outcome and level of satisfaction in life. If this sounds a bit ominous, don't worry because each choice is actually an escape route from misery. If you are at all unhappy, not just in your relationship but in any area of life, choosing one of these four options frees you. I'll break each one down and explain as we go, so let's start with the first one.

1. If you can't accept the problem, solve it.

Do you know how to solve the problem? Are you moving in that direction? Have you exhausted every single resource you can in efforts to find a solution? It might mean talking to professionals, searching online, asking friends and family that have been through similar situations, or other methods you haven't even thought of yet, just to say that you tried.

I worked with one client who never went to therapy, never told her best friends or family the truth about the emotional turmoil going on inside of her, and truly believed that there was nothing anyone could do to help her. She didn't think there was a solution, so she never sought one. I've seen this happen many times, where someone believes so strongly that they can't be helped, so they don't seek help.

I'll go out on a limb here and share this with you: Whatever is going on in your life, someone has gone through it before so never convince yourself that there's no solution just because you haven't found it yet.

There's no doubt that there are unresolvable problems in the world. You could have a rare illness or chronic pain and believe you've tried everything to cure and heal yourself. But have you? Or have you only tried things that were within the confines of your belief system? For quite a few years, I didn't want to believe in or acknowledge EFT (see page 50). To me, it was absolutely ridiculous that tapping on your body would heal or cure anything. But one day, for fun, I tried it on someone and magically, they felt better. I thought it was all in their mind (psychosomatic) and perhaps I was just very good at the power of suggestion.

Knowing I couldn't fool myself, I decided to try it on my issues. Fast forward a few years, and I now use EFT when I've tried everything else because it just seems to work regardless of my belief in it! I still don't understand it fully, and it doesn't work on everything, but I resolve to use it in spite of my critical brain telling me otherwise.

This is one example of seeking solutions that may be outside of your belief system. I've met quite a few "energy healers" and had never considered getting healing from them. After all, it's not logical, makes no sense, and is probably just a scam. Then one day a friend of mine offered to do it for me because she was studying to get her certification in a particular energy modality. I said, "Sure, what have I got to lose? I'll try anything once."

She came over, did some things with a magnet on my back, read some material out of a book, did some more magnet work, then two hours later, she was done. I thought, "Well, I'm glad I didn't pay for that!" However, over the following two days I couldn't get out of bed. I wasn't sick; in fact, I felt fine. But I was extremely worn out, as if I had no energy to move.

No energy...

My analytical mind was racing. "Could this be related to that energy session from yesterday?" I'd never felt that way before and hadn't felt that way since, but *something* happened. I could only point to that session as the culprit. And after those two days of much-needed bedrest, I was back to normal. The funny thing is that even though I still don't believe in many energy-healing modalities, I am still open to trying them out. If you can be receptive to possible solutions that may not fit your model of reality, you will have a much better chance of finding a resolution to your problem. Whether you search for someone else experiencing what you're experiencing, or you find a professional that works with the kinds of problems you're dealing with, there are almost always more solutions beyond your normal thought processes.

Expanding your knowledge and keeping your mind open is a great way to help you discover more solutions to resolve the problems in your life. With the Internet as an information powerhouse, you can find almost anything nowadays. Realize that if you absolutely cannot accept a problem in your life for whatever reason, you must do whatever it takes to solve it. Of course, you can know of a solution but may not have the strength, courage, or determination to go through with it. Or maybe you'll find that the problem doesn't actually have a solution! When that's the case, and you and those you've looked to for help have no clue how to solve it, then what do you do?

2. If you can't solve the problem, adapt to it.

"Adapting" means making the best of things and doing what you can to get through the day knowing that "it is what it is." You might say, "that's life," then move through that life without being too bothered by things you cannot change. You end up figuring out a way to be okay.

And figuring out a way to be okay can be powerful.

I had a sciatic nerve problem for over 15 years, the last few of which were the worst. After trying everything I could afford to get rid of it, I finally realized that there was absolutely nothing I could do to put an end to the pain. I hated that. I did not want to accept that I would be in chronic pain for the rest of my life. I couldn't even imagine a future where I would never know what it was like to be pain free. I didn't want to accept it, but I did find a way to adapt to it.

Adapting is sort of like acceptance because you know the problem won't go away, so you aren't in denial that it exists. It's also an acceptance of your capabilities and limitations. Normally I wouldn't tell you to accept your capabilities as they are, as I know that you have it in you to achieve great things in life. I also know that you are powerful beyond measure. However, if you've tried and tried but just can't seem to get beyond your circumstances, maybe you should accept that you have your limits and that you can't always win.

I realize how defeating and demoralizing that sounds! But there's something that happens inside when you finally give in: You stop fighting. When you're in a constant struggle trying to change what can't be changed, it gets exhausting. Pretty soon you'll just wear yourself out and feel powerless. By letting go of the struggle, you actually regain some of your power because you are no longer resisting what is.

The feeling of defeat can often be quite liberating. It can also allow you to think more clearly so that you make decisions from a new place, where you aren't so desperate for a solution. Going into a problem without desperation takes all the pressure off, and you tend to think more clearly. When I was suffering with sciatica, I just wanted to be out of pain and would do anything to make that happen. I felt the pain, suffered, complained about it, moaned and groaned, and did whatever I could to stop it. But by choosing to believe the pain was never going to go away, ever, and that I better adapt to it if I planned to have any kind of satisfying existence, I decided to embrace the facts about my condition:

⇒ I am in pain.

⇒ I have limited mobility.

⇒ I cannot do many physical activities.

⇒ Sitting makes it worse.

⇒ It will never go away.

Previously, I did not want to accept these limitations (especially the last one). After all, accepting them meant that I would have to suffer forever. But when I finally did give in and accept all of these things, the suffering stopped. Sure, I still felt the pain, but the drama that used to accompany the pain was no longer there. I didn't get stuck in my stories and complain to those around me who'd already heard it a thousand times. I just embraced the facts and accepted an undeniable truth.

Stopping the resistance stops the suffering.

Knowing there was absolutely nothing I could do to get rid of my pain, and that I just had to live with it no matter what, was actually somewhat relieving because I could finally stop focusing on it so much.

Adapting is a level of accepting. It doesn't mean you stop looking for a solution, nor does it mean that you really want to keep the problem. It just means you become okay with what's happening in your life and let go of your resistance to it. It's like telling the universe, "Bring it on. I don't care anymore!" Letting go of resistance is a path out of suffering. It doesn't solve the problem, but it clears the path for other solutions to appear.

Think about that in terms of relationships. How can you adapt to problems that you and your partner have? How can you work with a challenge because "it is what it is"? Can you even get to that point? If not, you might be a little upset that I even suggested it. But that's good! I want you to access some of those deeper emotions because they will cause you to take action. And maybe the action you take is exactly what helps you out of a problem. And that lines up with the third choice. If you can't accept or adapt to the problem, maybe you just need to get away from it.

3. If you can't adapt to the problem, walk away from it.

That means getting out of a situation, or leaving the relationship, or quitting that job, or removing yourself from anything that is causing you strife and struggle. If something is just so intolerable to the point you can't handle it anymore, you might need to get away from it even if just for a while because a temporary reprieve is better than none at all.

That's what my ex-wife did. She found my judgmental behavior to be too much for her, so she decided to walk away. She tried to accept and adapt but simply couldn't, so she walked out. And after a few months on her own, she realized just how much better she felt being away from the problem (*me*). When she was completely alone without my presence in her life, she knew she had made the right decision.

We're told that absence makes the heart grow stronger. I would change that to "absence makes us realize what we truly want in our life."

When my stepfather left my mom, giving her alone time that she'd never experienced before, she found her power again. She felt so free and started thinking more clearly than ever. I was worried at first, because it took her about two months before she realized that she even had the strength and courage to be without him. It was in her all along, but her mind was so tired and worn down that she couldn't access that strength while they were together.

> **An abused mind does not realize its own capabilities**
> **as long as it stays in the abusive situation.**

When that strength and courage kicked in, she knew that she would never be in another abusive relationship again, with him or anyone else. This was so different from just a month after he left, when she was actually considering taking him back. She had lived with him for so long she didn't know any other life than one with an abuser. It was like she was still under his spell, even though he was nowhere near her.

Several months after he left, she couldn't believe she ever wanted him back. She realized that she had become comfortable living with a dangerous person. This is how the abused mind works: It becomes more tolerant of abusive behavior until there is very little it won't tolerate. And soon even a slap in the face isn't scary enough to leave.

After some time without him as an influence in her life, her true, unclouded thoughts arose and she felt empowerment for the first time since she got married. My ex-wife probably felt a similar feeling after she left *me*, as she was finally able to think clearly once she was away from my judgmental eyes.

Getting out of an unhealthy situation gives you clarity. It's a powerful step toward clearer thoughts, and it gets you closer to the resolution of a problem faster. Sometimes walking away isn't the direct solution, but it often leads to a solution that you hadn't previously considered or thought possible. I've been offered more opportunity and money from every job I walked away from, reinforcing that very concept.

When you've had enough, sometimes you just need to get away from the problem, but many times in the face of walking out, you learn about new opportunities. The real bottom line is that the healing can start and you can begin looking at everything from a different perspective. That's something you don't have while you're still in the thick of things.

Walking away isn't giving up; it's honoring yourself by taking you out of harm's way. When it comes to relationships, walking away can be about honoring your partner by showing them tough love. After all, sometimes we have to do things that might make the ones we love unhappy even though our action is in their best interest. Getting away from a situation is sometimes the most healthy solution for everyone, even if the other people involved don't realize it or believe it. When there are other people involved in your unhappiness, they may need to be away from that situation too in order for healing to start in them. They may not even realize how much they contribute to the problem.

If, however, you've determined there's no way to walk away from the problem, for example chronic pain or illness, or you fear walking away from what you've invested your time and energy into, and you'd rather find a way to make things work no matter what, maybe you just need to accept things as they are.

4. If you can't walk away from the problem, accept it.

This is where you come full circle. If you haven't been able to make any other choice in the matter, this is where a choice is forced upon you. By selecting none of the other three choices, you are instead choosing to repeat the pattern and suffer. In other words, you're making "suffering" a choice. However, if you choose to believe that suffering is optional, and that making one choice could reduce or eliminate your suffering, how would you choose then? How would life be different?

Swiss-American psychiatrist and author Elisabeth Kübler-Ross once said, "The most beautiful people we have known are those who have known defeat, known suffering, known struggle, known loss, and have found their way out of those depths."

There is a path out of suffering, but it does involve conscious effort and maybe even bold action. Believing that suffering is a choice could be what makes the difference between miserable and manageable, or even enjoyable.

When you can't accept, adapt, or walk away, you put yourself in an endless loop of suffering. Sometimes you don't even want to consider what it would be like to accept, adapt, or walk away, but it's important to do so before you commit to any path. You want to avoid that endless loop.

Here are some questions to help you do just that. Put some thought into each just to see what you come up with.

➧ What would happen if I accepted that the problem as something that will always exist?

➧ What would happen if I adapted to the problem and just found a way to work with it?

➡ What would happen if I walked away from the problem?

➡ What is going to happen if I do nothing? How will life be for me?

You might have come up with some very enlightening answers to these questions. When you consider each one, does something shift inside you? Can you feel which question is the most powerful? Do you know which question feels the most "right"?

Did anything else come up for you while asking those questions to yourself? Questions like this can help direct you to the choice you need to make for you. Many choices we make in life affect other people. And typically, their behavior changes when ours changes. Imagine how other people would respond to you if you'd been suffering a long time, then one day you weren't. They may not know *how* to respond to you anymore! They may have gotten to know you as the person you always were, so they learned to respond to that person. Often, we want others to change so that our problems will go away. But if you are waiting for someone else to change, you will delay your own healing and growth. In fact, you could be waiting forever.

FOCUS ON YOUR HEALING, NOT OTHERS'

If the problems in your life have to do with a relationship, and you blame the other person's behavior for everything that's wrong about it, you will always have relationship problems. The quality of your relationships are directly reflective of the level of dysfunction in yourself. When you look at someone else who you believe to be the problem, you sometimes fail to observe what it is in you that keeps that problem in your life.

Whether it's a friendship, familial relationship, or romantic relationship, one of the biggest mistakes you can make is to focus on how to fix the other person without their asking for help. Many times the underlying reason you want to "fix" someone else is so that you will feel better. Sure you are compassionate and don't like to see your loved ones in pain or in danger, but if your intention is to fix them and not genuinely help them, you are likely doing more damage than good.

Wanting to fix or take care of someone else is a very parental trait. It can work in a relationship where you have to be a caregiver to someone who can't take care of themself, but when you're both responsible, self-sufficient adults, living with caregiver/caretaker roles isn't always the healthiest scenario because it creates codependent relationships.

Codependency (a scenario in which a "rescuer" meets his or her emotional needs in someone who needs rescuing, and vice versa) rarely results in a satisfying, fulfilling relationship for both people. In fact, what usually happens is that the person receiving all the support, attention, and care is very happy not having to worry or be accountable for anything, as the caregiver becomes more and more miserable every day.

The caregiver feels like they have to help the one with the "problem," believing that by doing so, the other person will eventually get healthier and become more of an equal. But what almost always happens in this scenario is that the rescuer, or enabler, becomes *more* accommodating, *more* tolerant, and *more* jaded and unhappy over time. This creates a massive imbalance in the relationship and very often leads to resentment.

Many dysfunctional relationships are set up this way. And a conditioning happens over time where both people become more comfortable in their roles. Even the enabler, as much as they can grow to resent their role, becomes *comfortable being uncomfortable*. This happens because the enabler doesn't want to let go of hope, so they keep submitting to responsibilities they believe they're obliged to carry out.

Holding onto hope that things will change is exactly what will keep them the same and actually cause them to get worse.

This is why it's so important for someone who feels like they are suffering in a relationship to seek their own path and stay focused on what they need to do to become happier and healthier. If you spend your time hoping the other person changes, you won't do anything to change yourself, and you'll attract the same problems again in the future.

HOW HOPE CAN BACKFIRE

I held on to the hope that my wife would change her ways. My faith that she would heal and get healthy again kept me from looking inward to determine if there was anything I needed to work on. I knew as long as I could hold on to hope, everything would get better eventually. But hope created a false reality of what was happening in the present moment. Hope can create a scenario where you deny things are bad and unhealthy and need to be addressed.

Does that mean hope is bad? Not necessarily, unless you are using it to hide yourself from truths you don't want to face. In fact, hope can get you through some very hard times in life, but try not to rely on it when history proves otherwise. In other words, the past is a great way to gauge future events. The past reminds you what will change and what won't. And it's typically safe to assume whatever you once hoped would happen but didn't is going to happen again the same way in the future. That in itself sounds very defeating, but it's not meant to be. Knowing how the past worked out, time and time again, gives you an opportunity to do something different the next time around.

Have you ever worked for a company and waited all year for a raise, and maybe even a promotion, but got neither? You might have chosen to speak up and ask why. Or maybe you chose to stay quiet because you thought that speaking up would get you disciplined or even fired. So another year passed and you waited and hoped once again that this year would be different than the last and that they'd finally recognize all of your hard work and dedication by giving you the wage increase you so deserved. But once again, another year went by and still you received no rewards for your hard work. You might have felt unvalued and underappreciated.

> **Hope encourages your belief in chance, but
> don't see that belief as truth until it is.**

Whether you've experienced that at your job or not, you can probably relate in some way. After all, how many times in your life have you put a lot of effort into something in hopes for a reward or some sort of payoff in the end? Many years ago, I decided to collect Hot Wheels and Matchbox cars—not for fun, but for profit. I looked up online auctions and found out how much the cars were going for, especially the older models, and realized I might be able to make quite a good side income.

I knew my mom always found the best deals going to yard sales every weekend, so I decided to ride with her and start my new venture. Soon, I was paying $10, $5, and even less for boxes of toy cars of all types. She and I visited many yard sales over several months and gathered hundreds of cars, both antique and modern. I knew that I'd at least get my money back and then some, but hoped I would be rolling in dough very soon.

Finally, I took inventory of everything we had and started looking up prices for each car. I separated the most valuable from the rest and decided to sell those worth the most in their own auction. I figured that I'd get at least a couple hundred dollars for these, as they were the rarest. I set them up side by side, took many pictures, and listed them on the auction site. I starting the bidding very low to garner interest and hoped that two or more buyers would want them so badly that they'd bid against each other until one of them finally stepped out.

The final day of the auction arrived and I sat there at the last hour wondering why no one had bid yet. Knowing the action in most online auctions happens in the last few minutes, I patiently waited until someone *finally* placed a bid. I thought, "Yes, this is where the frenzy begins!" Then I watched the clock tick down to the last 30 seconds. Then 15. Then zero. No one else bid; there was no frenzy. And because I set the initial price so low, that one bidder won the auction at my starting bid of nine dollars.

Months of buying, gathering, and planning, of hoping to cash in and be rewarded for all my hard work, came to an end with a nine-dollar profit. And you can't even call it a profit, because I spent much more in gas money gathering those cars. It was a total loss and I felt completely defeated. I set myself up for failure by banking everything on one idea, then relying on the hope that everything would just work out for the best. Has anything like this ever happened to you? You put your heart and soul into a business, relationship, or project, then discover it was all a big waste of time?

IIII **EXERCISE** IIIIIIIIIIIIIIIIIIIIIIIIIIIIIIIIIIIIIIIIIIIIIIIIIIIIIIIIIIIIIIIIIIIIIIIIIIIIIIIIIIIIIIIIIII

Has Hope Ever Backfired on You?

What did you invest a lot of yourself into that turned out to be less than you hoped for? Do you have feelings of regret, sadness, or anger about it today? Write down your thoughts and feelings below:

_____

_____

_____

_____

IIIIIIIIIIIIIIIIIIIIIIIIIIIIIIIIIIIIIIIIIIIIIIIIIIIIIIIIIIIIIIIIIIIIIIIIIIIIIIIIIIIIIIIIIIIIIIIIIIIIII

Most of my work with coaching clients involves hope (directly or implied), especially when it comes to their relationships. I've heard the following words many different times in many different ways:

➡ "Maybe he won't leave if he sees how much I love him and that I'd do anything for him."

➡ "I know if I am a better husband, she'll stop lying and staying out so late."

➡ "Today he wasn't mean to me, maybe this will be how it is from this point on."

My mom held on to the hope that her husband would stop drinking and treat her well. After 44 years, her hope that he'd leave finally materialized. A few months after he left, she suddenly realized that she had wasted all those years waiting for him to change instead of taking action to get herself to a better place. All she needed to do was look at the past to determine what was going to happen in the future. She didn't need a psychic to tell her exactly what would happen in a month or a year because she already knew. He never left before and was never going to leave. Sure, after four decades of waiting he finally did, but I wouldn't say waiting and hoping worked in her favor. She spent a big part of her life living with someone who abused her.

I spent a good eight years hoping my wife would change her behavior, but all that did was lead her to resent me and keep me from looking inward so that I could get the help I needed. It wasn't until she left me that thoughts I didn't know I had arose, and for the first time I found out what my truths were without her influence in my life. Her absence gave us both the opportunity to discover what we really thought about the relationship without either of us affecting the thoughts of the other, positively or negatively.

DON'T WAIT FOR THE RELATIONSHIP TO HEAL ITSELF

Sometimes change can't happen until you are away from what influences you most. If you're in any type of relationship or situation where there have been no changes or progress in the last 3, 6, or 12 months, there will be no progress in the future either. And even if you can't prove that's not true, believing it's true may be enough to move you from hope to acceptance.

The hardest step to take can be the acceptance of truth. If you no longer have hope that someone else will change, you have to accept that they won't, which brings you to seeing a reality you may not want to face.

> If you cannot accept someone else's behavior, you need to either heal yourself so that you can accept it, or honor yourself so that you are no longer a part of it.

It's quite possible someone in your life may need help and healing where you can tell what needs to change but they can't. They may do behavior that you don't like, but should you step up and try to help them even if they don't ask for it? Quite frankly, even if you have the perfect solution for them and think you can actually fix them in some way, it's not your problem. It is a problem in the relationship for sure because it affects you, but it's their problem, not yours, and they need to take their own steps to resolve it. If one of those steps involves asking you for help, then by all means step in if you'd like and do what you can to help them. But it's not always in the other person's best interest for you to offer your guidance when it isn't asked for.

I'm not referring to ignoring an elderly person trying to change a flat tire by herself, or looking the other way when you see a child reach for dangerous utensils. There are real moments where jumping in to help is absolutely welcome, and could even be lifesaving.

I'm referring to a condition or emotional state that someone is in when they do behavior that you don't agree with, or when they cause a problem in their life or yours. If you're a "fixer" like I'd been for many years, you'll likely want to step up and offer many solutions just so you can resolve the problem and move on. But sometimes the other person does not want a solution from you. In fact, if you jump right into fix-it mode, they may feel like you're not listening at all and like you're even invalidating their thoughts and emotions. It could make them think you really don't care about their pain, that you only care about fixing the problem—even if helping them resolve a problem could be your way of showing love.

Often it's best to show that you care by just being there if they need you. Trying to tackle their problems and make them yours isn't always healthy, and can even be quite damaging to the relationship. It's important to let the people in your life deal with their own problems in their own ways for two reasons:

1. The changes are likely to stick. If they come to a solution them-selves, the changes will likely hold indefinitely because the steps they took toward that solution were self-initiated. Changes that you initi-ate for yourself almost always have a greater chance of lasting. In fact, when you get to a point where you can't stand how things are anymore and you decide to make changes in yourself, it's a very empowering sensation. It's like taking control of your life again. And since being in control is a nice feeling to have, you are more likely to keep the changes you made.

2. There is no resentment. It's a lot harder to accept someone else telling you that there might be something wrong with you and that you need to change. This is especially true in relationships where you place a greater value on your being right. And if someone else, even gently, insists that you make changes because they can't handle your behavior, that might be even less of an incentive for you to make those changes. It can build resentment in you because even if you do change your behaviors, you will probably always feel as if you were coerced or controlled in some way. It may even seem like your free will was taken away.

This is why it's so important to focus on yourself when you notice things you don't like in others. The idea is to observe a behavior that bothers you in someone else and ask yourself, "How can I come to a place inside of me where this behavior doesn't upset me?"

This almost sounds as if you're saying it's okay for the other person to do "bad" behavior, but that's not what this is about at all. This is really about honoring yourself to the fullest. Focusing on you helps you heal and make decisions that are right for you. This allows the other person to focus on themselves so that they can make decisions that are right for them. When both of you come to that empowering place inside, and you are both on a path of healing, you can either come together happier and healthier, or move away from each other knowing that you've made the right choices. Healthier decisions are almost always made after healing.

CHOICES ARE SO MUCH EASIER TO MAKE WHEN YOU'RE EMPOWERED

Unfortunately what happens too often is that one person makes changes and finds healing but the other doesn't, so the relationship doesn't improve. In fact, when one person heals, if the other isn't healing and growing themselves, they may end up getting left behind. When you are mentally stronger and emotionally healthier, you tend to desire the company of people that are on a similar path. As you leave behind some of your old dysfunctional behavior, you'll find that your selection of friends and romantic partners evolve.

There are less people you'll want to spend quality time with as you move into a new, healed space in yourself, simply because there are less people that have "done the work," so to speak. Personal development is a journey with a lot of hard realizations and leaps of faith. When you are the type of person that takes those leaps, you'll find that you want to be with others that are also willing to take similar steps to become healthier people.

The next chapter is about becoming the person you need to be in order to attract the person you want to have in your life. If you already have a romantic partner and aren't planning on changing that, you can still get a lot from the next section. This entire book is about self-empowerment, especially in all the different types of relationships you're in. Once you are empowered, you make the right decisions for you. After all, there will always be challenging people in your life. And who you show up as will determine what results you get. If you feel empowered to make decisions without fear and honor your boundaries no matter what, you're going to be much more prepared than most people.

Who you attract and who you are attracted to is almost always a reflection of what level of personal growth and development you've reached inside of you. If you're hurt, you tend to seek those that are more nurturing. If you are needy, you'll be attracted to those that are more giving. If you are the one that is more giving, you'll likely attract and be attracted to people who want to be taken care of (but not always in a healthy way).

So whether you're currently in the greatest relationship of your life or thinking about starting a new one, let's get into what it takes to create strong, loving bonds with mentally healthy people so that you don't have to give up who you are in the process.

CHAPTER 6

How to Avoid Attracting the Wrong Partner

For some strange reason, immediately after my divorce was final, I thought it would be a great idea to start dating again. The same old program started replaying that convinced me that happiness comes from being in a relationship. I was feeling down in the dumps and convinced myself that finding the next "perfect" relationship was the solution to my blues.

So I signed up to an online dating site. In fact, it was the same website I used to find my wife eight years previously. I figured I had good luck then, so maybe this time I'd have better luck. Also, I enjoyed the process of receiving new prospects in my email inbox every day so I knew what to expect, and figured that I'd eventually be happy once again when I found that perfect someone.

Anticipating lots of prospects, I was surprised when very few appeared in my inbox. I thought the problem might be because I was choosing to look in my local area only. But I decided to give it some time. Two weeks went by and only a handful showed up, none of whom looked appealing to me. I got somewhat disappointed, so I decided to join a second dating site. After all, I really wanted to get this "happiness" thing going again so I could get my life back in order.

After another two weeks of that, I had a couple of conversations, but nothing panned out with anyone on either site. I started thinking that the dating scene had changed and that finding someone wasn't going to be simple as it was before. I was hanging on to the belief that a month was enough time to find the perfect woman, and I was growing impatient.

After a couple more stale weeks searching for the woman of my dreams, I started asking myself questions like, "Am I just not attractive anymore? Do I look pathetic in my pictures? Is my profile turning the right people off and only attracting the wrong people?"

I started to think that I needed to up my game again. I thought, "Maybe I need to expand my criteria to the entire United States instead of just my local area. And maybe I need to change the age range I was seeking and be a lot looser in my other requirements."

These thoughts and more about how I could further manipulate the system to get additional prospects started running through my mind. I felt myself getting a little obsessive trying to make this dating thing work out for me once again. No one's profile grabbed me and said, "You need to meet this woman now!" So my desperation started to build and I got more determined to make it work.

As some hopelessness started to creep in, I suddenly became aware of that desperation and I didn't like the way it felt. I had done so much personal growth before my divorce, so I thought I was over a lot of the negativity in my life. Desperation felt like a huge step backwards. I thought, "Is it normal to feel so desperate?"

Desperate didn't sound very healed to me. In fact, it sounded dysfunctional! The next thought I had was, "Am I placing all the responsibility for my happiness on someone else?" I had a real concern that I might be so buried in desperation that I might not be discerning enough when it came to choosing a good potential partner. I stopped and asked myself, "What the hell am I doing? I'm getting ready to jump right into another relationship when I haven't even healed from the last one." I had what some might call an *epiphany*. I realized that this is the exact same road I'd taken after every other breakup, and I was about to do it again.

As always, I was searching for someone else to take the full responsibility for my happiness, which is a very tall order. For the first time I considered how much pressure that puts my partner under. I thought, "How would they ever be able to live up to that?" The thought of that struck me so hard that I had to sit down and contemplate it for a while. I remember thinking about how challenging that must have been for my partners over the years and started to feel regretful and even a little guilty. I thought, "How is it normal to expect someone else to make me happy?"

This thought process caused some sort of shift inside my head. I was learning something new about myself and I wasn't sure how to process it. As the gears turned, I came upon another major discovery about myself: I've never been single!

I have been in some sort of relationship since I was 18. I've never been alone long enough to experience life with just me. That concept was absolutely foreign. I never explored what life would be like without someone else because I was always too busy trying to meet someone or keep someone. In fact, I couldn't recall the last time I had a thought that wasn't somehow influenced by a romantic partner because I've almost always had one or thought about getting one.

If you're in a relationship right now, think about the following questions for a moment:

⇒ Does every thought you have include your partner in some way?

⇒ If you chose to leave the house and take a drive for an hour or two, would you wonder what your partner might think about that?

➡ Can you finish off anything you want in the fridge without worrying what your partner might say?

IIII **EXERCISE** IIIIIIIIIIIIIIIIIIIIIIIIIIIIIIIIIIIIIIIIIIIIIIIIIIIIIIIIIIIIIIIIIIIIIIIIIIIIIIIIIII

Here's a Test

Would you do or say anything different if your partner didn't exist? If you're in a relationship, write down one thing that you would do differently:

_____

_____

_____

_____

If you're not in a relationship, write down one thing that you wouldn't necessarily be able to do anymore if you got into one. (For example, "I won't be able to play my country music as loud as I want at 3 AM")

_____

_____

_____

_____

There are always pros and cons about being in a relationship. I have a good friend who went through a divorce and said he was pretty much done with relationships. He seems quite content now, living in a house by himself and not having to worry about going to sleep at a certain time or having dinner ready or having to check in with anyone about anything. That's not to say he won't date or meet someone new and change his mind, but he is enjoying being with his own thoughts for now.

Every thought I've ever had while in a relationship included my partner in some way. Even when I go out with my friends, enjoying my "me" time, I'll still have thoughts such as:

➡ "I wonder if she wants a snack while I'm out."

➡ "I wonder if she'll be mad at me if I stay out too late."

➡ "I can't hear my phone, I better check to see if she called."

The list of thoughts that include our partners in some way can go on and on. Even after a breakup, we are typically still influenced by their existence in the world as if we were still together.

I came to that realization. My ex-wife was still in my mind and almost every thought I had was influenced by her in some way. This was a big wake-up call, because I had no idea that my focus was only on either getting her back or getting someone new. It was never about being single. And because of that, I got those desperate feelings that made me unhappy. It was a dysfunction in me I didn't know was there.

In retrospect, I now understand that I had no idea what life was like without being in an intimate relationship of some sort. I hadn't yet experienced solitude in my environment, let alone in my head, because there was always someone else there. After realizing this, I needed time to heal from my former way of thinking so that I could experience and understand myself on a whole new level. I wanted to make decisions based on nothing but my own thoughts and let go of the idea that I needed to be in a relationship. I especially wanted to end this stupid feeling of desperation and figure out who I really was without anyone's influence in my life, whether in a relationship or not. Nobody, including me, knew who I was because I was never without someone else.

When you don't know yourself well enough to share who you really are with another person, you're going to attract or be attracted to someone that may not be the best choice. In fact, they could be downright unhealthy for you if you haven't yet taken the time to find out who you are and what you still may need to heal inside of you. Remember, you'll often attract partners that need a similar level of healing as you, so you are more likely to date dysfunctional people if you yourself have more work to do. This doesn't mean you should never date until you're healed, you just want to process and heal as much as possible so that you can attract more amazing relationships.

THE DYSFUNCTIONAL FEEDBACK MACHINE

Learning about your dysfunctions and what you bring into a relationship can be really eye-opening and educational. Your partner not only reflects in you what might need healing, but they are also a wonderful dysfunctional feedback machine. Their dysfunctions feed your dysfunctions, yours feeds theirs, and you both perpetuate the cycle.

I worked with a woman who would hurl passive-aggressive comments at her boyfriend, and in return, he would fire some back at her, which kept the feedback machine running. In other words, it took one person to start the process and the other to perpetuate it. The good news about that is that it also takes only one person to stop the process for the machine to break down, but unfortunately, this rarely happens. Typically, both people are attached to their position and won't budge. In the case of my coworker, neither she nor her boyfriend even realized they were being passive-aggressive toward each other, they just knew something was wrong. In its most basic form, passive aggressiveness is repressed anger expressed in such an indirect way that nothing is ever discussed or resolved. No wonder they couldn't figure out how to resolve their problems, as they actually never expressed them clearly.

Imagine you were angry that your partner never did the dishes. Instead of saying, "I am angry you never do the dishes. I feel disrespected as if you don't care about me," you say something passive aggressive, like, "I would serve you dinner if there was a clean plate, but it looks like there are none as usual!" This type of comment is indirect anger. It's completely unproductive and usually leads to deeper resentment because the real issues are never brought out into the open to be discussed. And if you both continue feeding into unproductive communication like this, the dysfunction and building resentment will never end. In this example, the only way both of you could heal and move forward is to get out of each other's proximity for a while and rediscover what life was like without the other person in your life. It could be a short vacation or a few days with family, but if you stay in that type of environment and neither of you is willing to back down, it will only continue to be painful.

There are ways to stay together and work through these things, and certainly counseling would be extremely revealing and helpful, but if you are unhappy and triggered more often than you are happy, something might need to change, at least temporarily. I encourage temporary separation when there is enduring dysfunction. When you're in a system that functions because you're *in* that system, you may need to remove yourself from it so that you can reset and reflect before jumping back into it. Separation will give you the space and time you need to learn about what you really want in your life, and also heal from the emotional wounds you might be carrying around. Emotional triggers are a wonderful gift to let you know there's more work to do, though they are rarely seen as gifts in the moment.

The Dysfunctional Feedback Machine works marvelously well and cannot stop until one component (you or your partner) chooses to stop feeding into it. A temporary reprieve from each other gives you both enough time to reflect on how you treat each other, how you treat yourself, and what you can do differently when you're together.

It can be more challenging to reflect on your own behavior when you're constantly being triggered by the other person.

EMBRACE BEING SINGLE

When I was ready to start dating again immediately after my divorce was final, I was fortunate to come to the conclusion that it was way too soon and I was not far enough along in my healing process to consider that option. On top of that, I knew that because I was eager to find someone new in my life right away, I was approaching dating the wrong way. I was going into it with a desire to replace what made me happy instead of wanting to share the best of me with someone else. Because of that, I was at risk for ending up in yet another dysfunctional relationship. The solution to all of this was to embrace being single, cancel both online dating accounts, and start life over again without the pursuit of romance. When I made that decision, I felt really good about it. I thought, "Wow, I'm actually not going to pursue another relationship. This is so strange to me!" I couldn't believe I was actually happy that I wasn't going to be in another relationship. I felt *empowered*.

If you really want to avoid attracting the wrong partner or keeping a partner that isn't healthy for you, first embrace that it is okay to be single. Even if you're in a relationship now. To come to a place where you are absolutely prepared to be single no matter what, you'll find that most of the stress you had in your previous (and current) relationships was more about not losing the person you're with instead of being the best you can be for both you and them. When you're so focused on doing everything you can to keep someone instead of doing everything you can to heal and grow inside yourself, you tend to become more unhappy over time. The best type of relationship is one where someone loves who you are inside and out so much that all they want for you is to be happy. This is a person who honors your honoring yourself, and will even support you if you don't want to be with them anymore. It's not easy to show this kind of love for someone, but if you define love as I do (supporting the other person's happiness), and if being with you makes them unhappy, then loving them means supporting their decision to leave you.

Being or becoming single isn't a death sentence. I used to think it was, but it turns out that time alone is time to heal. Letting go of the idea that being single is bad will empower you to make decisions based on what's right for both of you in the relationship. I remember my first long-term girlfriend getting to the point where she simply didn't love me anymore. I was a wreck! Her words to me were, "It's just time." Back then, my only goal was to prove to her that we could make this work. I didn't honor her path and wanted to fulfill my needs only, so I begged her not to go. I tried to convince her to stay and that I'd change.

If that happened to me today, of course I would be hurt. But I would also realize that once someone reaches that point, it's better to honor their path and let them come to self-empowered decisions. That way, they won't resent you for talking them out of a path they chose to follow. The only way to prove to anyone that you're a keeper is to focus on yourself and do whatever healing and growth you need to do. Over time, if you truly are the right person for them, you are going to shine when they look at you. The idea isn't to do it to impress them, though; it's to become a better you for *anyone* that comes along.

And if you are ready for the next relationship, it's a good idea to figure out how to determine if a potential romantic partner is good for you as opposed to one that is "bad." Have you ever created a list of your must-haves and must-not-haves for a relationship? If not, it's a good idea to do that so you can be clear on what you want. Use the space below to make a list of the qualities that would make an ideal partner. Even if you're already in a relationship, just write down what the ideal relationship looks like. Coming up with these criteria will help you understand what makes you happy and what causes you strife. I'll start you off with an example:

My ideal partner must… be honest with me even if it might hurt, respect my opinion, call me out if she knows I'm wrong, like intelligent conversation, etc.

My ideal partner must not… drink excessively or smoke, abuse me in any way, disrespect my friends, etc.

This is very similar to the values exercise from Chapter 2. If you've already listed your values in relationships, you can skip this part. If not, do the exercise and see what comes up for you. After, we'll talk about how to go about attracting that ideal partner.

|||| EXERCISE ||||||||||||||||||||||||||||||||||||||||||||||||||||||||||||||||||||||||||||||||||||||||

My Ideal Partner Must…   My Ideal Partner Must Not…

_____   _____

_____   _____

_____   _____

_____   _____

_____   _____

_____   _____

_____   _____

||||||||||||||||||||||||||||||||||||||||||||||||||||||||||||||||||||||||||||||||||||||||||||||||||||||

ATTRACTING THE IDEAL PARTNER

By the time I met my current girlfriend, I had made a commitment to stay single and there was no inner desperation kicking in. I didn't feel like I had to impress her or anyone.

We'd made contact online just before I permanently disabled both of my dating accounts. I told her about my decision to stay single and why. I also wanted to share with her just how unappealing I was by telling her the unfiltered truth of where I was in my life at this time. In a small way, I was *trying* to be repelling. I knew I had nothing to lose by being honest (after all, I wasn't looking for a relationship), and wanted to be authentic from that point on. My new life had started and it was time to find out who I was when I wasn't trying to filter the truth from people. I told her I had just gotten a divorce, moved across the country to live with my mom, and started a business that was making no money. I told her I needed to experience what it was like to be single for a while. I chose to be brutally honest, wanting absolutely no false notion that I had any interest in her or anyone at this time of my life. Plus, I had never experienced what it was like to be 100 percent truthful about myself. In the past, anytime I started dating anyone, I did what I could to only show my best side. But then, having made the decision to be more authentic and figure out who I was without anyone else in my life, I made it my mission to honor *me*. I knew she'd run away screaming once I told her the raw truth. However, the next day she wrote back:

"LOL, it's so refreshing to meet someone on here that's actually honest. Thank you for that..."

Then she shared where she was in her life and talked about her divorce many years previously. I couldn't believe she wrote back. I thought, "Who would want to converse with someone who has all these problems?" I expected that being authentic would drive people away, not make them more interested.

That was the first of many exchanges with her, or anyone, where I chose to be completely honest and vulnerable. Having a history in the same field of work, we kept our conversation and shop-talk going through private emails and eventually on the phone. It felt liberating to talk to someone that I could share anything with without trying to impress or convince them that I was a great catch. I felt completely free to be myself with her because I had no hidden agenda, nor any desperate longing for someone to fill a void in my life. My choice to be single freed me to show up as myself.

A happy relationship is absolutely possible. In my case, I eventually moved out of New Hampshire to be with her, and it was a great decision for me. We are both committed to speaking our truths and expressing ourselves *no matter what the cost*. If you can get to that point and be honest, even if you believe your partner will be upset or leave you, you will be able to form a powerfully strong bond that will continue to grow stronger over time. The reason for that is because you develop trust in each other even though there are some hard truths to face. It's a great feeling knowing that your partner is telling the truth, even when you don't want to hear it.

"Hard truths" are those deep realizations in yourself that you are afraid to share with those you love. My ex-wife taught me this concept before we got married. In the first month of our relationship, she was staying over at my house. I was in the bedroom and she was in the kitchen. I was cleaning the room along with some music. She yelled something to me from the kitchen but because the radio was on, I didn't hear her. There was a song I liked so I turned the volume up. A few seconds later, she came into the room and looked at me with what appeared to be a little sadness and anger. I immediately turned the music down and asked her what was wrong. She said, "When I asked you to turn the music down and you turned it up, I felt very disrespected."

My eyes got wide because I realized what just happened. She was trying to yell to me from down the hall to turn the music down, but because I didn't hear her she thought I turned it up in spite of her wishes. She felt I was being disrespectful. I apologized profusely and explained what happened. She was fine almost immediately but I learned a valuable lesson that day. I wasn't used to someone expressing their upset in a way that wasn't accusatory. She didn't come in yelling and telling me how bad I was. She also didn't repress her anger and not say anything. She just checked in with herself to comprehend the situation and figure out what she was feeling, then expressed herself to me.

I felt really bad that she took it that way, but I also learned that I was with someone who wasn't going to hide her emotions. She was going to present them to me so that I could process them and talk about it. She gave me a chance to hear a hard truth, one that could have led to an argument or some other heated conversation. After all, telling someone you feel disrespected by their behavior, especially when you don't know how they'll respond, can certainly be a challenge.

Hard truths are what you typically want to hold in and not share because of your fear of what might happen if you do. But the more open you are with your hard truths, the less you repress or hold on to negativity. Getting hard truths out in the open is certainly a leap of faith, but when you and your partner can talk about and overcome them, the trust and bonding will usually get stronger. Not always, however, as some hard truths are so hard that your partner may not be able to handle them. If that's the case, it's better to find out sooner than later so that you both know if a healthy, honest relationship is possible.

A relationship that allows hard truths is one that becomes more resilient and more real than any other relationship you've experienced. The more you show up as your authentic self and speak honestly about what's going on inside of you, the more your partner gets to see and love the real you. That kind of relationship where you are both bringing your truths to the table lets your partner know they can trust you, even when what you have to share may not be what they want to hear.

SHOWING UP AS THE REAL YOU

Do you show up as your authentic self in your relationships? If not, why not? Sometimes the fear of what might happen can override your authenticity, and you may feel like it's better to hold back instead of express yourself. When that happens, you become someone you're not. And that can lead to a breakdown of your happiness, an increase in stress, and an eventual burnout, because you will get exhausted.

It's not easy to not be yourself!

In fact, you expend a lot of energy when you choose to repress what you really think and feel all the time. In relationships, do you try to show only your best side to your partner or potential partner? I did that for most of my life. I really believed the best side of me to show was the one I thought other people wanted to see. I believed the real me would never be good enough to stand on its own.

Showing up as the real you will always work out better than the one you think the world wants to see. It's not only easier for you (because you don't have to hide), but it builds stronger bonds and longer-lasting relationships. So many people are not authentic and end up in relationships that end badly. Save yourself a few heartbreaks and *just be you*. Of course, if you're carrying around some emotional baggage, maybe you're not too fond of the person you've been for all these years and don't want to be you. If that's the case, then do the best you can and hope things work out.

Hope things work out? Well that's a dismal outlook! But there is a reason I say that. When you're serious about improving yourself and healing from old, emotional wounds but just can't figure out exactly what needs to heal, a relationship is a great trigger to start that ball rolling right away. After all, your partner knows you best, and they will behave in such a way that highlights where you both need improvement or growth. In other words, your partner is the perfect reflection of your level of healing or dysfunction.

Sometimes the wrong partner is exactly what you need to attract the right one later. This sounds like it is almost in direct conflict with the previous section, where I talked about embracing being single so that you will have the time and space to grow and heal. But there comes a point where you aren't sure what your next step is. Before my girlfriend and I got together, I felt like I'd done all the healing and growth I needed. It was only then that I chose to get into a relationship. I even remember telling her once, sort of jokingly, "I'm completely healed! I'm ready for a relationship now." She laughed.

I admitted that I probably have a lot more healing to do, but I honestly couldn't figure out what else I needed to heal from. Since there was no one in my life acting as a stimulus for my triggers, I didn't know what my next step was. Sometimes the next step is to get into a relationship and see what happens! Both terrible and terrific relationships are always feedback for what you need to work on in yourself. Fortunately, the worse a relationship is and the more you're willing to learn and grow from it, the better your relationships can get. That's if you're willing to learn from your experience and take with you the lessons gained.

"Bad" relationships are the catalyst for change within you and will only have meaning and purpose if you choose to learn and heal from what created those circumstances to begin with. It doesn't mean you caused the problems that arose, but it does mean taking responsibility for what you choose to allow in your life from that point on. When you leave a dysfunctional relationship, you are either going to take with you the person you were (the one who didn't see all the red flags in the previous relationship), or the person you want to become (the one who knows you have some healing to do and will see red flags in the next relationship early on).

There's no doubt that no matter how emotionally healthy you are, you can still get into relationships with emotionally unhealthy people. Some partners don't reveal their true colors until months or years later. That's why it's so important for you to come into any relationship with a level head, balanced heart, and clear understanding of your personal boundaries. Be aware of your feelings because you'll always know what's right and what's not. That way when your partner crosses the line, you can address what's happening right away.

This is absolutely vital: Let your partner know when they've crossed a personal boundary so that you give them a very clear indication of how the relationship will continue. If they apologize and never do what they did again, the relationship has potential to be amazing. If they convince you that your boundary is wrong or that *you* are wrong somehow for having it, you'll need to make a big decision about the future of your relationship. If you choose to let things slide, your level of toleration will rise and will crack the door open for another boundary violation in the future. Then when they cross that same boundary again (or another boundary altogether), you can choose to let it slide or not. However, be very careful when allowing violations like that in your life.

> **The more you allow your personal boundaries to be violated, the more tolerant you get of abusive behavior.**

As your toleration level rises, you start to develop an *abused mind*. The abused mind reaches higher and higher levels of toleration to the point where it soon calls any abuse "normal." This is why it is so important to walk into a relationship with a firm grasp of what you will and won't allow. There are times when you can be lenient for sure, and sometimes you might find that you are simply too stringent on some things. Other times you'll discover that you no longer need a particular boundary anymore so you'll just let it go. In general, enforce your boundaries whenever possible. When something doesn't feel right, it may be time to stand up and honor yourself.

Remember to ask yourself: "Is this right for me?" When it doesn't feel right, make a different choice. This is truly what honoring yourself is all about.

WHEN RELATIONSHIPS GO WRONG

What you haven't healed from will show up in your relationships.

When you feel any type of emotional deficit, as if something were missing from your life, you might find yourself seeking that in someone else so that you can feel "complete." If you have been neglected, abused, or traumatized in any way, it can feel like a part of your life was ripped out from under you. Growing up and moving out into the "real world" as an adult, you may find yourself seeking what's missing in you from others. This typically creates codependent and other types of dysfunctional relationships. You don't have to have gone through any sort of trauma to experience something missing in your life, but it's typically more prevalent when you have.

When you don't believe you have all you need within you to attain happiness, you will always be searching for that happiness from someone else. When you are seeking happiness from a potential romantic partner, you can develop an unhealthy dependency and that desperate feeling I talked about earlier. It's healthy to want and enjoy love and attention from someone else, but if you correlate being in love with your happiness, then when you're not in love, you won't be happy. You can see how this might be a problem when you're not in a romantic relationship because you'll have no one around to "make you happy." This can also occur when you're *in* a relationship but things aren't going so great. If your partner has become more distant or less connected to you, it feels like happiness is that much farther away.

Love and happiness can certainly go hand in hand, but they should be able to exist individually as well. Being in love gives you the feelings of comfort, security, significance, and a whole lot more that you might label as happiness. There's nothing wrong with that label, as long as love from someone else isn't your only source of it.

A relationship can be one of the most fulfilling experiences of your life because it amplifies everything you want and more. It can also be a total disaster and one of the hardest, most painful life experiences. That's because you become heavily invested in the relationship and your partner—you have in it a lot of time, energy, resources, and even money. If you *really* want a stellar relationship, address the dysfunction in you first. I addressed this before, but it's so important to realize that everything you are triggered by in your partner is a reflection of what needs healing in you. When you stay with someone that continues to trigger you, either you need to heal or they need to stop the behavior you don't like. If they don't stop their behavior, then whether you stay or go, or heal or don't, determines whether or not dysfunction in your relationship continues.

Remember, dysfunction is just a term to indicate that something isn't functioning well. When you haven't healed from some sort of emotional wounding from the past, you bring dysfunction along with you on the path of life. This causes you to experience unwanted stress, unneeded anxiety, and add more demand and worry to your already overwhelmed brain. A dysfunction might be when you become involved with someone that showers you with gifts but you go into denial that they are a compulsive liar. Or like the dysfunction I carried around with me for over 35 years: I felt that my partners had to change to accommodate me. When they didn't change, I would judge them until they did or until they left me. Dysfunction eats away at both of you and erodes your happiness to the point where you're no longer loving each other, you're only tolerating each other.

The only good thing about dysfunctions in relationships is that they are presented to you as opportunities to learn what you need to heal in yourself. Your partner will trigger dysfunction in you, and whatever insecurity, fear, or any other negative emotion or behavior comes up will be the emotional wound that needs your attention. Your partner doesn't necessarily trigger you on purpose (although sometimes they do), but they are usually in their own dysfunction when they are acting in a hurtful way.

For the longest time, I was very needy and dependent on my partners for my happiness; therefore, I was always attracted to loving, nurturing, and overly-giving women. At the same time, those same women were attracted to me because their need to give love, support, and attention to someone in need was being fulfilled. A codependency like this can work great for the first few months of the relationship, but it starts to get old within the first year because the enabler realizes that the one in need isn't getting any better. In fact, that person usually gets worse and even *more* dependent as the helper accommodates them. This is exactly what happened to me. As I was being nurtured and cared for in my marriage, I was enjoying how my wife accommodated me and how no matter how harsh I was, she would continue to love me. I grew more dependent on her compassion. This allowed me to embrace my dysfunction and stay exactly where I was.

As you probably already know, this is unhappiness waiting to happen. The challenge when two people get together is to make sure they complement each other in a positive, productive way instead of a negative, dysfunctional way. Every one of my former relationships was based on dysfunction until I realized that I was searching for what was missing in me. When you're seeking what's missing in you from other people, that puts them in the tough position of being your source of happiness and fulfillment. No one can ever fill that role completely, so you end up with a relationship that can never be good enough. And even when it's great, if you are unhappy when they're not around, the relationship as a whole suffers because having that responsibility can drain the other person's energy.

WHEN RELATIONSHIPS GO RIGHT

One of the worst ways to start a relationship is when you use the other person as a means to fulfill what you feel is lacking in you. Like I said before, we tend to seek in others what's missing in our life. That might sound a little repetitive, but it's an important concept to understand so you don't get swept away in what seems like a perfect relationship that then turns into a disaster later.

However, knowing that you have to heal yourself if you want to attract a healthy partner doesn't mean you have to wait forever. After all, are we ever truly healed from everything completely? We are all imperfect beings that have work to do on ourselves, so we can't just let life pass us by while we continue our personal growth and development journey.

It is just as important to be with yourself as it is to be with someone else. A friend, family member, or romantic partner can always be there as an objective observer and let you know what they see in you that you can't necessarily see in yourself. This feedback can be valuable and help you change or heal what you may not even know is there. Often, a good partner can be there as a supporter of your healing process, but it takes a very special bond to keep that going. If you are both supportive and respectful of each other's journeys, a lot can be accomplished because of the trust that's been built between the two of you.

There are times when all the energy in the relationship needs to go in the direction of one person, as that's what the give and take in a healthy relationship is all about. You may hurt yourself, so your partner focuses on you to help you through it. Your partner may run into some financial difficulties, so you focus on them. The relationship becomes dysfunctional when one person decides that the problems that arise are caused only by their partner, not themselves. When one person takes no responsibility and shifts much of the blame and responsibility on the other person, it's no longer a safe, loving, supportive environment. It can even become toxic.

I had a female client whose husband was manipulative. He didn't believe he needed any help, and she was always left feeling guilty after every conversation or argument they had. He had become masterful at using words as covert weapons to make her feel bad. He never said anything that directly blamed her for their relationship troubles, but somehow she kept getting it in her head that all their problems were her fault.

His focus was always on her and how she needed to change. Even when it was clear that he did something bad or wrong, he found a way to turn it around and make it her fault. This is a clear example of what it means to shift all the energy and blame on someone else instead of taking any responsibility for your role in the problem yourself. There are many types of manipulators in relationships, but most of them have the same qualities when it comes to blaming others for everything and taking no responsibility.

A healthy relationship is one where both partners actually want to work on their own healing and growth and not the other's. It "goes right" when you find someone who supports your journey and you support theirs. It's a matter of learning what makes them happy and supporting that happiness as much as possible.

When I met my current girlfriend, she made it clear that no one got between her and her friends. I thought it was quite an unusual statement to make, as I had no intention of interfering with her friendships. However, this is exactly what had happened in her past relationships, so she decided to make it a clear boundary up front; that way, I would be certain that crossing it would spell big trouble. After we started seeing each other regularly, not only did I not interfere with her friendships, I encouraged her to see her friends and talk with them as often as possible. After a few months, she realized that I wasn't there to interfere whatsoever. In fact, she came to understand that I only wanted to support her path, not veer her from it. Had I discouraged her from spending time with her friends, I would probably have been kicked to the curb long ago.

Another example of supporting someone's journey is something my wife told me when we were married. During a particularly troubling time of our marriage, she pointed out how her uncle treated his wife. At the time, I was judgmental and got triggered by her behavior often, to the point where she became more and more depressed. She told me how much she wished I was like her uncle. She said that he's been married to the same woman for years, and he is happier than ever. I wanted to know what their secret was. The answer she gave me became imprinted in my brain and started my journey of healing. She said, "My uncle said, 'I don't care if my wife gets old, ugly, or fat, all I want is for her to be happy.'"

When I heard that, I felt a sudden sadness and guilt arise in me. The years that I'd been with my wife, I'd never had that thought. I never wanted her to just be happy...I wanted her to make *me* happy. By the time I really adopted this philosophy, my wife had fallen out of love with me and was on her way out. But I refused to let this new lesson slip by and it became one of my values in relationships. From that point on, I made a promise to myself that I would always support the happiness of my partner, even if that meant they would be happier without me.

That is a huge declaration to make, as it might involve a big sacrifice on your part. But if you stand by that philosophy and follow it always, you'll have much more amazing relationships. That doesn't mean you support them dishonoring your boundaries or lying to you; after all you still deserve the same treatment back. But adopting this as a way to treat your partner and remembering this one statement, "I just want them to be happy," will help you make the right decisions for both you and them and give you both a partnership that you want more than ever.

HOW YOU PROLONG DYSFUNCTION

Sometimes getting the "right" relationship involves becoming aware of where you might be going wrong. When there is dysfunction in your relationship, it can keep you both in a constant triggered state, causing you to feel bad most of the time. However, sometimes you're so embroiled in the thick of relationship issues that you can't even tell where dysfunction begins and love ends. It might make you wonder why you stick around in a relationship that has so many problems. There are many reasons why you might stay with an unhealthy partner, but I want to give you a chance to reflect a bit on a few questions that might give you some insight on what you are or aren't willing to allow in your relationship.

Do You Keep Toxic People in Your Life?

These questions are mainly for introspection to help you understand where you are and why you might keep (or not keep) an unhealthy or toxic person in your life. Look at them as "what ifs," and imagine how you might answer if they were true.

➡ If you found out that your partner lies to you, would you keep that person in your life? If so, why would stay with a liar?

➡ If your partner decided that they'd rather not help around the house at all, would you keep that person in your life? If so, why would you stay with someone who makes you do all the housework?

➡ If you saw your partner abuse your pet, would you keep that person in your life? If so, why would you stay with an animal abuser?

➡ If your partner disrespected you, maybe even in front of your family or friends, would you keep that person in your life? If so, why would you stay with someone who disrespects you?

➡ If you discovered your partner had a private phone you didn't know about, would you keep that person in your life? If so, why would you stay with someone who hides things from you?

➡ If your partner hit you in anger, would you keep that person in your life? If so, why would stay with someone who abuses you?

These are harsh questions, I realize, and there is no right or wrong answer to any of them. There may be multiple reasons you'd stay with someone who did any of these things. The questions are worded in such a way to emphasize one thing: you are responsible for honoring yourself in a relationship, not changing the other person.

|||||||||||||||||||||||||||||||||||||||||||||||||||||||||||||||||||||||||||||||||||||||||||||||||||||||

When you can fully embrace that concept, you will never have to carry the burden of their dysfunction on your shoulders. I once had a relationship where the girl I was with stole from department stores. I didn't know she was doing it and only found out when we got stopped by store security one day. Confused, I followed her and the security guy back to his office, and my girlfriend starting removing stolen items from under her shirt!

I was like, "What? You stole?" It was embarrassing, and I wondered for how long she'd been doing it. The question that might apply to me is, "If your partner steals from stores, would you keep that person in your life? If so, why would you stay with a thief?" Today I can answer that easily, but back then I couldn't. I did stay with her because she stopped stealing immediately. Of course, we talked about it and had to grow through it, but everything was fine after that. However, if faced with that same scenario today, and if my girlfriend said she wouldn't stop stealing (and didn't want therapy), I would have to remember that I need to honor myself in the relationship and not change her. I'd *want* to change her, but if she didn't want to change, I would need to honor me. Had I honored myself many years ago when my girlfriend was caught stealing and if she refused to quit, I may have left the relationship. Even if that meant giving up all the time and energy I'd invested into it. That investment is typically the reason many people don't leave bad situations. They feel like they put a lot into it so they'd better stay and suffer instead of plan an exit.

Sometimes you can talk to your partner until you are blue in the face and they still won't change—or can't. That's when you pull out The Four Choices (page 76) and come to a conclusion. If you can accept who they are, dysfunctions and all, then it's no longer a problem. And you might be able to find happiness in the relationship after all, though that is unlikely if they are violating your boundaries, as in an abusive situation. Or you might even discover that your inability to accept their behavior is a dysfunction in you, and choose to work on yourself instead of focusing on them.

Near the end of my marriage, I finally realized that our relationship issues had nothing to do with my wife's eating addiction and everything to do with how I *responded* to her eating addiction. Her addiction was hers to deal with, not mine. But I made it mine and wanted to fix it. After we separated, I woke up to the realization that my inability to handle her addiction was the real issue in our marriage. I asked myself, "How much of a problem would this be in our relationship if I was able to love and support her regardless of her struggle with food?"

The answer that came to me was that her struggle was not a problem in the relationship at all, it was a problem in me. As soon as I embraced that, I took responsibility for my behavior. I chose to heal me by doing whatever it took to focus on myself and what caused me to judge the ones I love so harshly. It was a journey that freed me from my own emotional prison.

This is a question you can ask yourself too when you need to figure out just where to focus your time and energy when it comes to relationship issues:

"How much of a problem would this be in our relationship if I was able to love and support my partner regardless of their behavior?"

There are, of course, behaviors that *should* be unacceptable to you, and you need to honor yourself if your partner does those behaviors. That might mean standing up and expressing yourself to them or maybe even leaving them. You should enforce your standards and boundaries that go unmet or are ignored or you will be unhappy. However, maybe your answer to the question above changes that perspective. The idea is to keep as much dysfunction out of the relationship as possible. The more you allow, the more unnecessary suffering you may go through.

The bottom line is that if they do behavior that is not acceptable, something needs to change. Since we can't change others, we can ask them if they will. If they can't or won't change, then what happens next falls back on us.

THE PULL GAUGE

Whether you're in a relationship now or are thinking about your next one, use what I call the "pull gauge" to help you determine the best way to approach it. My girlfriend introduced this concept to me. She said if she felt drawn or "pulled" to be with someone, she took things very slowly. She kept her guard up and became very aware of their behavior, what they said, how they said it, and how they treated other people. Even though she might have felt attracted to the person, that didn't always mean they were a stable or emotionally healthy partner.

When she felt no pull to be with them, she was more at ease. There was no pressure to impress and she could let her guard down a little. She noticed that she was able to determine someone's true nature when she wasn't drawn to them and held under their spell, so to speak. When you feel that pull toward someone, you may not see red flags that may be there. You might be continuously drawn to them and think about them all the time. However, you might also not see how badly they treat their parents or maybe you'll be less likely to question why they can only talk to you on Tuesday nights after 11 p.m.

There's typically a pull with any type attraction, healthy or not, but when you feel it, be aware that you may be less observant of other signals. Feeling the pull of someone else to draw you closer to them seems like it would be the most natural effect of love or attraction. But while you're drawn to them, you tend to lose focus of some of the important aspects of you and what you need to honor in yourself.

Being drawn toward someone isn't necessarily a bad thing, it's just a powerful state that can cause you to put the blinders on.

I was once drawn to a woman I worked with so much so that I couldn't think straight when I was near her. However, I was already in a relationship, so this was not healthy behavior. What made it worse was that she was drawn to me too. Attraction can sometimes be so powerful that we do things that we regret. Fortunately, I was able to take control of my behavior and pull myself back. I knew that any further contact with her would only lead to bad news. She never made a pass at me, but I didn't want to take the chance at making a big mistake by being near her again.

This type of attraction can happen whether you're in a relationship or not. It's alluring and provocative, but it can limit critical thinking and keep you from making appropriate choices. When you want to create a healthy relationship, don't base your decision on the pull. That's one component of a bigger picture which includes your boundaries, values, beliefs, likes, dislikes, and more. It's also helpful if the other person isn't already in a relationship! But when they are available and you want the opportunity to build a healthy, long-lasting relationship with them, just be aware of any pull in you. The pull is a good signal to take it slow before you take bigger steps into a deeper connection.

In every relationship I've ever gotten into, I would follow my partner wherever she wanted to go. When I felt the pull toward them, I didn't question anything, I just followed them like a puppy. This could be the behavior of a hopeless romantic. Many love stories are built on the premise of following your heart; however, what the stories don't usually tell you is that following your heart isn't always the best course of action. Sometimes there are other factors involved that need to be addressed before you jump in with both feet. You don't want to end up with someone who you are extremely attracted to but also does behavior that goes completely against your values or boundaries. Taking it slow, having a lot of conversations, and asking a lot of questions before getting too deep with them keeps you from being driven solely by the pull you might feel. This is very hard to do if you're used to following your heart. That's not to say your heart isn't involved, but it's better when every part of you—your heart, mind, and body—can get on board before taking the big leap into love.

Don't let desperation or pull cause you to jump into a relationship with your eyes closed.

FOCUS ON THE RIGHT PERSON

The best relationship is the one where you are free to express everything you are, even at the risk that your partner might leave you. Many couples, however, do the opposite. They suppress who they are out of fear for the same reason. This causes one or both of them to act in a way that they believe will please their partner, sometimes at the cost of honoring themselves.

When you are in a relationship where your partner has his or her needs met to the detriment of yours, it is unbalanced, unhealthy, and cannot sustain love. If they do not reciprocate by fulfilling your needs too, then by staying in that relationship you may be dishonoring yourself. Giving to someone who doesn't give back creates a one-way street where deep connection decreases and the rift that forms between you increases.

If you express your truths—those honest, sometimes scary-to-convey thoughts—even at the cost of your partner being upset with you, you will strengthen the love and bonding between you. Not every relationship can withstand this kind of authenticity, of course, because it takes a lot of trust (which is something that can take time to build), but when you find one that does, you will experience no greater connection. It is one of the keys to a healthier you and a more enriching, rewarding relationship.

When you are on a path of self-growth and healing, and you are with someone who is also focused on the same thing, you can create a wonderful, expressive, and strong relationship. If, however, you choose to focus on what's wrong with the other person and how you can help them change, there will start to be a decline of power on both sides. Trying to help other people change when they haven't asked for your help is focusing on the wrong person. You might be able cause them to change temporarily, if at all, but they could develop a resentment toward you.

You know how it feels when someone tells you what to do, right? You can sometimes feel controlled and manipulated. It's disempowering and it doesn't feel good at all. If you really want someone else to change their behavior or beliefs, don't tell them what to do, *work on yourself*. One of the secrets to a happy relationship is when you honor you. By doing so, the other person in your life will pick up on it and can choose whether they want to go along with you on that journey or not. By honoring yourself and doing what's best for you, you bring the best version of you into the relationship. When you make changes, your partner can choose to make their own changes or not. When you focus on yourself, not only are you on a self-empowering path but you give your partner the freedom to choose their path too. It's possible they may not choose the path you're on, in which case that "freedom to choose" falls back in your lap. The freedom to choose what?

The freedom to choose whether you want to continue a relationship with someone who has different values and ideals than you. It doesn't mean your partner is a bad person, it just means they have different aspirations. And you need to decide if you can travel on the same path with both of your unique perspectives. Typically what happens is that the person going through the personal growth and development phase outgrows the one who isn't growing at all. And both of you will experience a divergence in the relationship until one finally either leaves or changes their behavior. If neither of you change, then things will stay the same. If you're happy with how things are for you now, this is a good thing! If not, then you may need to take the first step toward self-improvement and hope your partner follows. If they don't, either or both of you might have to decide whether to stay together or not. The ultimate goal is to grow what you have into a great (or better) relationship, but *it* doesn't move until you or your partner make that move.

When you want to improve the relationship, improve yourself.

If you really want to experience a different type of relationship, one that is more than what you may be going through now, focus on yourself. You can't really change anyone but you anyway, so don't waste too much time arguing, complaining, or telling your partner what to do. They're either going to choose to do it or not, but it has to be self-initiated from an empowered place within them. Otherwise it won't stick. You always want them to come to their own decision if possible. If they ask for your opinion, it's still initiated by them and can be just as empowering. You can offer input or guidance at that point, but try not to dig too deeply into their problems otherwise. The bigger picture is always their own free will and personal empowerment so that no ill feelings ever build against you. That's one of the most ideal environments for a relationship to flourish.

Staying in a relationship where free will is taken away or manipulated in some way is moving away from satisfaction and fulfillment. In a case like that, you may have to leave, which could create the best scenario for both of you. That way, you are no longer being offended or disrespected, and your partner gets to learn what happens when they do bad or unacceptable behavior (accountability). There's also, of course, the other option of accepting bad behavior, but why would you want to do that?

If you have no choice but to accept bad behavior due to circumstances beyond your control, you may just have to wait it out. Sometimes their behavior isn't necessarily intolerable, but it might be something you don't want in your life. For example, one of my first girlfriends smoked cigarettes. I was never fond of smoking so I insisted that she never smoke around me and that she also brushed her teeth before coming to see me. She had no problem doing this and I appreciated it. Eventually we broke up. I think back now and realize I never wanted to be with a smoker in the first place. She wasn't a bad person, but she did "bad" behavior in the sense that I could not accept it in my life (in other words, it was bad for me). The breakup wasn't pleasant but it was good for both of us, because now she could find someone that didn't mind her smoking and I could find someone that didn't smoke. I still cared about her but sometimes you don't want certain behaviors or personality characteristics in your relationship, so you need to take care of yourself and honor what you want for you.

Another example of not accepting behavior is with a client I once had whose boyfriend spent more time playing video games than paying attention to her. She eventually chose to leave the relationship because his "bad" behavior—playing more video games than spending time with her—was not something she wanted in her life. The behavior itself is not bad, but it was not right for her and the type of partner she wanted.

If your partner does behavior that is not acceptable to you, doesn't plan on changing anytime soon, and you don't plan on coming to a place of acceptance with it, you may need to start planning your escape route. After all, you deserve what you want in a relationship. I know someone who waited eight years before she finally found the right partner for her—let's hope she keeps me!

Plan in advance exactly what you're going to do if and when you need to leave. If the person you're with does really bad behavior (for example, if they are violent or abusive) then plan carefully and reach out to one of the many support organizations out there. They know the drill and can help you get your thoughts straight and take the safest path for you. Hopefully you're not in a situation like that, but know that you are not alone if you are. Go to your local library if you have to so that you can do your research covertly.

"Bad" behavior isn't necessarily a reason to leave a relationship but it certainly doesn't make it any more enjoyable. In fact, you might be in a situation where nothing bad is happening at all—it's just time to move on. That's what my first long-term girlfriend said as our 13-year relationship was coming to an end.

She had fallen out of love with me and there was nothing left for her. I had plenty more to give but she didn't want it. She just wasn't fulfilled anymore. She didn't have the energy to continue with it, so it ended. I was heartbroken but no amount of convincing would have mattered because the love simply faded. Unfortunately this happens a lot to couples that aren't expressive and honest and have trouble communicating their truths to each other. There were so many times I wanted to tell her how angry I was but chose to repress that anger instead. I believed that by showing my anger she'd recoil in horror and not want to be with me. Instead, she unconsciously sensed that I was holding back my true thoughts and feelings, and that wore her down over time because she never really knew what I was thinking. She could never connect with me at that deep level I wanted because I was too afraid to show her my true self and express those hard truths.

There are so many ways a relationship can unfold, so it's important to always continue working on your own personal growth and healing whenever possible. That way when you look back on everything that happened you can say you tried your best. Continue to work on yourself and do whatever you can to bring the best you into the relationship. Having a partner do the same for themselves usually creates the best outcome, so hopefully they are on the self-improvement path too.

Get to know your values in relationships by doing the exercise in Chapter 2. Learn what's most important to you so that you can gauge whether you and your partner (or potential partner) are on the same page.

A relationship is the sum of what both people put into it. Learning your values and coming into alignment with those values reveals exactly what will make it great for the both of you. Keep your focus on healing and growing yourself, and be as honest and expressive as possible. If you suppress your thoughts and repress your emotions, you'll create a dishonest environment. You may think you're creating a peaceful situation by not telling each other your hard truths, but if both of you are committed to making the relationship work, the hard truths are almost always better off expressed. It's better to get them out in the open for discussion than to have them fester within to become an angry outburst or explosive conversation later.

A great relationship starts with an empowered you. And when you are in that space, you'll make better choices and won't be attracted to the same people you once were. If you find yourself attracting mentally unstable or emotionally unhealthy people, look inside you and explore what's missing in your life. It doesn't mean you're unstable, but it might mean that what attracted you to them is something you're not aware of in you.

For example, I attracted an addict into my life whom I ended up marrying. Since I was brought up by an addict in childhood, I realized I tied addictive behavior to love and happiness. Learning this about myself, I was able to dig into it further and heal what attracted me to that personality type in the first place. Addictive behavior isn't bad in and of itself, it's just not a good fit for me. Learning this helped me be aware of what I was attracted to in others so that I could be more scrutinizing in my partner selection later. After my divorce, I decided to make a commitment to stay single until I felt healed enough to get into another relationship. I also wanted to be happy being alone so that I didn't pursue anyone out of desperation. If that meant I had to stay alone while on a healing journey for the rest of my life, I was willing to take that journey.

Are you willing to go the distance with your own healing and growth? Be authentic. Be the real you. It's not only about expressing your truth and walking your talk, it's also about showing vulnerability without fear. And vulnerability can be very powerful. You may have some emotional trauma to heal from before you're able to become vulnerable, but when you get to the point where you can approach the world with confidence in your vulnerability, you'll have almost everything you need to become the emotionally healthy, authentic, expressive person you want to attract, so stay with me as we dive into the next chapter and talk about it. Vulnerability is a place of power that can cure insecurities and build emotional strength and resilience in almost every part of your life.

CHAPTER 7

Build Emotional Strength by Being Vulnerable

> When you are comfortable being vulnerable, you will have
> all the emotional strength you need to achieve anything.

It's hard to believe that vulnerability builds emotional strength, because the very thought of choosing to be vulnerable might make you think of feeling unsafe or unprotected. But if you think of strength as a feeling of assuredness, believing you can handle almost anything that comes your way no matter what, you might understand it more clearly. For example, imagine you have a fear of public speaking (do you even have to imagine it?), and you were asked to present on a subject matter you knew very little about at the last minute. Someone hands you a bunch of notes and says that you need to get up and speak right away. You have no idea where to begin and aren't even sure what the purpose of the talk is. Then the room starts to fill up and you are motioned to get on the stage. You reluctantly stand and make your way to the front of the room.

Very few people would be completely anxiety free at this moment. In fact, just picturing that, you may have gotten at least a little nervous in some way. If public speaking doesn't bother you, just think of a situation you know would cause you some angst. For the majority of people reading this book, fear of public speaking (a form of social phobia) is very real. The mere mention that you might be made to go on stage can cause all kinds of fears and insecurities to creep in. And the idea of getting in front of all those people, especially so unprepared, can leave you feeling vulnerable and exposed.

But how exactly is feeling vulnerable and exposed necessarily bad? Let's just say you went on stage completely unprepared and people started looking at you strangely. What if some of them started chuckling and others shook their heads in disapproval? What if many of them were simply waiting patiently for you to say something amazing? Standing up on the stage without any preparation or intrinsic knowledge of what you're presenting may cause you to feel a certain way.

What exactly do you feel?

In this situation, anxiety is one of the most popular answers to this question. And whether you feel that or something else, the next question is "Why?" Why do you feel that way, or why do you feel anxious? Most people would answer with one or more of the following:

⇒ I don't want to look like an idiot.

⇒ I'm afraid people will laugh at me or make fun of me.

⇒ I'm afraid they will see right through me.

⇒ Why would anyone want to hear what I say?

⇒ I'm not smart enough.

All of these answers can be very real to the person saying them, but how exactly are they a problem? And why wouldn't you want to feel that way? I realize that sounds a little crazy, but it's probably a question you never asked yourself. And sometimes asking yourself the questions you don't normally ask is a path to healing.

All of the above responses can lead to feelings of vulnerability and insecurity, but the real reason for that isn't exactly clear until we drill down a little into each one and define what they really mean to us. For example, let's just say your answer to "Why do you feel anxious?" was "I don't want to look like an idiot." If that were the case, I would ask you, "Why not?"

DRILLING DOWN INTO DEEPER MEANING

The answer may be clear to you: "Why not? Nobody wants to look like an idiot! What a stupid question." But if you and I were talking about this in person, I would drill down and find out what's underneath that answer and why specifically you have a problem looking like an idiot.

"Drilling down" is just a term I use to get more specific about the words people use to get past the generalizations they make. A generalization in this case could be the statement, "Nobody wants to look like an idiot!" I might drill down into that comment and ask you to clarify exactly what you mean by "nobody" and also find out why you wouldn't want to look like an idiot. If this seems strange to you, good! *Strange* can work in mysterious ways, so let's keep going with this concept.

The Drill Down process helps you discover where exactly fears come from. Many of us carry around these generalized fears without knowing where they come from or if they're even valid anymore. For instance, I used to fear losing my job. I feared it so much that I would do or say anything to make sure my job wasn't in jeopardy, even if that meant compromising my integrity. My excuse was, "I need the money so I can't lose my job."

That's a legitimate comment that anyone could make on any given day. But if we drilled down into that comment, we might find out that for me, it's *not* about not having money. It might be about something much deeper. For example, it could be about not feeling valued, or something more primal like not wanting to go hungry. But instead of using words like value or hunger, I'm using general, more simple descriptions to perceive my world and create fear inside myself. Most of us do this, as it makes communicating much more efficient. However, perceiving the world from this surface level viewpoint keeps us from having to face something deeper inside ourselves. We don't necessarily do it on purpose, it's just a faster way to convey our message.

When you have a fear that you've generalized to a comment like, "Of course, *anyone* would be afraid of that," instead of saying something specific and personal like, "I am afraid of that because…," then you're causing yourself to stay in fear instead of get beyond it. Generalizing specific fears that apply to anyone convinces you that it's normal to be afraid and that you'll always be that way. What I teach is that it's normal to be afraid *and* it's normal to discover what's beneath it in hopes to eliminate your fears altogether. It doesn't mean all fear inside you will disappear, but after reading this chapter, you'll have more tools to reduce it tremendously.

Living in fear is not a healthy way of life and can cause you to become ill and miss a lot of life events. But are your fears what you think they are? One of the reasons I ask, "How, specifically, is that a bad thing?" when it comes to what someone fears is to understand the meaning they give to that fear. When I was afraid of losing my job, I asked myself the question, "How is losing my job a bad thing?" The answers I came up with were the excuses that have held me back for years. When I drilled down into those fears, I found what I feared most wasn't about money or work at all. They were based on some lower-level needs that I was afraid to compromise. The work was a means to money, which was a means to food and shelter, which were a means to safety and security. The more I drilled down, the more I realized that the fear of losing the job wasn't the real fear at all. After discovering that, I was easily able to speak up for myself at work (something I had never done previously) even though I could get fired for what I was saying. In other words, I was empowered to say and do things that I felt were right instead of doing things out of fear. The fear of getting fired simply disappeared when I figured out what I was actually afraid of.

The Drill Down Process

When you fear taking steps toward something that might be better for you, you risk staying exactly where you are. That's okay if you like where you are, but if you don't… the Drill Down process will help you understand what specifically is causing your fears instead of the reasons you may have been using before. If you said, "I fear losing my job because I need the money," you might believe that the main reason for your fear is not having enough money. But is not having enough money your actual fear? Is not having enough money a direct fear, like being afraid of a spider or a snake?

When you are sleeping in bed at night, do you carry money with you? And if not, does that cause you to lay in bed with fear because it's not with you? Typically, most people would not be afraid going to bed without money. But I know what you're thinking, "I'm talking about money in my bank account, money that pays the bills!"

I get that. When I was married, I watched our bank account go down to zero. That was a very scary time for us. I wasn't afraid that I didn't have any money *on* me, I was afraid we didn't have any money, period! But when I ask you about not having money, I'm looking for a more compulsive response—the kind of response you get when you are surprised and scared at the same time.

I remember working in an attic one day with just a flashlight. It was tight, dark, and very hot because of the Florida sun. I was looking for a telephone cable and was trying to be careful not to step onto the insulation and fall through the ceiling. At one point, I turned around to look in another direction, and as I moved my flashlight, a giant spider appeared inches from my face hanging on a single thread of his web. I nearly jumped out of my shoes while falling backward. Fortunately, I did not fall through the ceiling. I pointed the flashlight up again hoping it crawled back up to the roof, but I noticed that it hadn't moved. Then I realized it wasn't moving at all.

Oh…it was dead.

I felt a huge sigh of relief knowing that I wasn't about to get attacked. A lot of people have a fear of spiders, so I use that story to describe something you are compelled to fear. A compulsive fear response is one that you experience at a very primal level, what some might refer to as a fight-or-flight response. I was surprised and scared at the same time. However, if I knew it was there ahead of time and wasn't surprised by it, I probably wouldn't have been scared at all. In fact, I might have just had a heightened awareness, but nothing more. My fight-or-flight response would not have kicked in.

Compulsive responses like the one I just described activate our defenses so that we do *something* to survive. We are wired to react and behave to continue our existence. But what does this have to do with the previous example of losing a job and being without money? That's where the Drill Down process comes into play. Think of drilling down as taking a concept or idea and figuring out the origin of that concept or idea. For example, someone didn't wake up one day and say, "I'm going to invent a phone!" Ideas existed before the phone was invented, so when it came to be, it followed a succession of events that made it possible.

This is how your thoughts, feelings, and emotions exist too. They have a previous event from which to draw. And the idea behind drilling down is to connect the dots from what you feel today to what your emotions are truly about from the past. Most fear is created in the past and brought with you through every event in your life. You carry around a lot of old fear that you think still applies to today's circumstances, but in reality, most of them probably aren't needed anymore. That's why it's important to drill down into your fears and understand their origins.

The moment I faced that spider wasn't an actual threat, but something must have happened in my past to make me automatically afraid of it. After all, if you saw a pink blob covered in chocolate chips and toothpicks on the floor, would you scream and fall back in terror? Probably not, because there's nothing in your past that indicates something that looks like that is a threat. However, with spiders, you might have had an experience that you can think back on that caused you to fear them. Even if you didn't have a direct experience, you might have been around someone that was afraid of them and saw how they reacted, so you learned that you should be afraid of them at that point. Obviously, this analogy doesn't work if you're not afraid of spiders, but just think of something you are afraid of and apply that same logic.

The fear that might come in to someone losing their job can be very similar to someone else's fear of spiders. It's a compulsive response that contains of lot energy. With a spider, there's the possible fear of getting bit in that moment. It's a more rational response, because you don't want to experience physical pain. But losing a job is not an immediate threat, so why would you react with any fear at all in that moment? You may not, but many people do. I lived in fear of losing my job for a long time but I never knew why until I learned this process. So I'm going to walk you through it so that you can apply it to things you're afraid of too, whether it's public speaking, fear of crowds, fear of quitting your job, or even fear of spiders. This process helps you uncover the real reasons you may feel fear in a given moment and may actually cause the fear to disappear.

IIII EXERCISE IIIIIIIIIIIIIIIIIIIIIIIIIIIIIIIIIIIIIIIIIIIIIIIIIIIIIIIIIIIIIIIIIIIIIIIIIIIIIIIIIIIIIIII

Decoding Fear

Are you ready? First, think of a situation you fear coming true. For example, losing a job or relationship, going broke, or something else that doesn't involve death (grieving has an entirely different set of variables).

Now answer the following questions:

1. Why do you fear that?

Think of all the reasons that come to mind. This is the first level of drilling down. Even if you think the reasons are silly, answer honestly. When you get an answer, go on to the next question.

2. What *about* that do you fear? What specifically?

This is where we start drilling down into a deeper place in your mind to get a better understanding of where the fear comes from. Don't worry if you can't answer these questions directly, just continue on to the other questions until you're done.

3. What other emotions are you feeling?

Fear is an emotion, but are you feeling anything else? Anger? Embarrassment? Guilt? Worry? Anxiety? It's important to identify exactly *what* you're feeling so you can answer the next question. If emotions are coming up for you, feel free to express them here and now. Give yourself some time to do so before rushing into the next questions.

4a. When was the first time you ever felt this kind of fear, or something close to it?

Look back into your past and search for a time when you felt these same emotions and fear that you feel now. Was there another time in your life that you felt this way? If so, what's the earliest memory you have of experiencing this emotion? If you're having trouble remembering the past, just be aware that those emotions stemmed from your past and have resurfaced today to give you an opportunity to process them.

4b. What exactly were you afraid of then?

This is where we get more direct responses that start to lead to some primal fears. Many of today's fears may come from a desire to be alive and exist. I call them "primal fears" because they are triggered as if your very existence were being threatened; they exist at the most basic level of survival. In most cases, having no money isn't an *immediate* threat to your survival. But you might respond to it as if it were, causing you to feel anxiety and other fears.

5. Thinking of your answer to 4b, how *specifically* is that a bad thing?

This question tends to throw people off, but really consider it. No matter how bad the event was that caused fear in you, *how* is it bad? Don't answer in a generalized way like, "everyone knows it's bad," because what's important to figure out is why it's bad for *you*. You may also want to follow this question up with, "How do I feel about it?" Sometimes the deeper stuff comes out here. Feelings of being unloved, unwanted, insignificant, unworthy, or afraid of pain can sometimes show up. What is it for you?

6. Again, thinking about your answer to 4b, is there something worse that could have happened than what did happen?

Think of the absolute worst-case scenario. Imagine what it would be like if what happened was worse than your experience. How bad can you imagine it being? When you think of what's worse, think of something else *even worse* than that. Be as creative as you can be and really experience how you'd feel if it happened.

If this step gets uncomfortable for you, just come back into the present moment and know that you are safe, because you can come back to this exercise anytime you'd like. I don't want you to go to a place that you can't handle. If you're ready and willing to go the distance so that you can get beyond this fear, stay with me and push through it. Soon you'll start to perceive the original event from question 1 a little differently. It's not that you're changing what happened, but it may change how you feel about it.

7. What could have happened that was even worse than the worst-case scenario you just envisioned?

Now imagine what might be even worse than before. Where does your imagination take you? How bad can it get? I know this is a tough exercise, because it's almost as if you are forcing your brain to imagine scenarios that could be unbearable. But, believe it or not, this is building a new level of emotional resilience in you.

Again, stop anytime this is just too much. I don't want this to be overwhelming; I just want to help you expand your mind in a direction you don't usually take it. There is a purpose to all of this. By imagining something worse, you are diving in beyond your original fears so that they don't have so much power over you. Sometimes we see a fear as something to avoid, as if it were the end of the road. Fear is a stop on the road, but not the end. There's so much more beyond and sometimes we need to stretch what we know to be true into an area that isn't true at all *just to have a different experience.*

This different experience, one that we are making up in our mind, is so radically different than the original experience that it alters our perspective of that original experience.

8. Think of your answer for question 2 again. What would happen if you were back in that original experience, in the moment of that fear, and suddenly you stepped outside of your body and

looked at yourself from 20 feet away? How does this change your fear?

If your perspective didn't change after considering the worst-case scenario, it will likely start to now. Usually when we're afraid of something, we see it the same way every time. These questions help you perceive what you believe to be true *differently*, so that you are not stuck with a single outlook. Adding new perspectives gives you new thoughts. You can imagine yourself 100 feet away or 1000, and you'll experience the event in an entirely new way.

9. If this fear didn't exist, how would your life be different?

This helps you realize there are different ways to feel. If you can't imagine what it would be like without that fear, then imagine what it would be like if other things related to the fear didn't exist. For example, if there was another person involved, how would your life be different if that person never existed?

It's another strange but enlightening perspective that gives you an opportunity to explore some positive space inside you and let you know that even though you may have fears, you have good feelings too.

10. Think about what you originally feared. How do you feel about that now?

Has your perspective changed? Do you feel better? Worse? What has changed? It's important to be aware of where you are with your emotions, especially the ones that tend to control your life. Awareness is the first step to processing and releasing what you don't want in your life anymore.

If nothing has changed or if the fear has gotten worse for you, do the secondary Drill Down process, which involves one question repeated over and over again:

What about that is bad?

Secondary Process

Do this exercise in the following way:

1.   Think about what you fear again.

2.   Ask yourself, "What about that is bad?"

3.   Whatever answer you come up with, ask yourself again, "What about *that* is bad?"

4.   With every answer you get, keeping asking, "What about *that* is bad?" and so on. If you really follow this through, you'll likely uncover a primal fear that might need addressing.

Eventually, you'll reveal that what you were originally afraid of no longer frightens you as much, if at all. The Drill Down process takes you inside your fear, breaks it down, and rewraps it so that you have a different understanding of it. If I were to do this with you in person, many more things might come up and the questions would probably be different. But the purpose of *drilling down* is to reveal the original emotion and maybe where it comes from, because what you fear today isn't what's happening today, it's what has *already* happened in the past to set that fear in motion.

IIIIIIIIIIIIIIIIIIIIIIIIIIIIIIIIIIIIIIIIIIIIIIIIIIIIIIIIIIIIIIIIIIIIIIIIIIIIIIIIIIIIIIIIIIIIIIIIIIIIIIIIIIIIIIIIIIIIIIII

I once feared going broke. I was so afraid that I'd have no money because I believed it meant I couldn't survive. But then the day came where I had no money, and I was okay. In fact, I survived for many months completely broke. I was fine. Life was harder, but I was fine.

Looking back, my surface level fear was about money. But my deepest fears were about how I was going to survive and if I was going to starve or not. What I've found more often than not is that most fears come back to that survival-mode thinking where even though in the moment you're okay, you might be accessing a low-level, lizard brain fight-or-flight response. For example, you might be afraid of losing your job because on the surface, it means you lose your income. But at the deepest level, you might actually fear death. And because of that, you have an overreaction to what could be considered a very non-threatening, though important, event in your life.

That's a massive jump in belief, I realize, but if you choose to perceive all of your fears as a fear of death, then let me tell you what happens: almost all of your fears might disappear. But it takes overcoming one thing and only one thing for you to get to that point, which I'll talk about in the next section. Drilling down into your fears is vital to getting them to release their tight grip on you. Responding to the world from a place of fear instead of empowerment only brings more fear. Getting to that empowered place takes leaps of faith, knowing that you'll end up happier and more fulfilled if you honor yourself instead of fearing the consequences.

The fear of consequences stops you from taking leaps of faith. Sometimes it stops you from taking even the baby steps of forward momentum because your mind goes into *what might happen* instead of *what you want*. If you stay in What Might Happen mode, you may never get what you want and you will always perceive the world from a fearful place. However, if you choose to stay in What You Want mode, you will do things that honor you and those you love and let the chips fall where they may. It can often mean the difference between happiness and unhappiness. There are levels to each, and the more you honor yourself and go for what you believe in and what you value most, the more happy you become, even if people don't like your behavior. The less you honor yourself and react to the world from a place of fear, the less happy you'll be.

The challenge is getting beyond the fear. Drilling down is one way, but there's another, more powerful way.

ACCEPTING DEATH AS AN OUTCOME

What if you had a belief system where you attributed every fear in your life to a fear of death? What would happen if you attributed the fear of being yelled at to a fear of death? How about the fear of how your father or mother will react when they hear the news of something you did? What about being late for work? What if everything you feared was really just a fear of death? It almost sounds ridiculous at first because there are so many minor fears that all of us carry around with us, so how could each one dwindle down to a fear of death?

Well, let's start by realizing that almost all of our fears started in childhood. When you were a toddler, did you know what you feared and why? Most likely not. If you remember that far back, you probably didn't think of fear the way you do now. When you're born, you just want to get your needs met. We are all hardwired to pursue our most basic needs. If we don't, fear will drive us to get them met. When they're met, we're happy. When they're not, we're unhappy. Unmet needs may not start out as fear, but they do transform into fear after we become a bit more analytically minded.

The baby crying for food isn't necessarily afraid, but the baby that never gets fed does feel pain. Over the years, that pain morphs into fear, which spreads into all areas of life. As you grow up, food usually doesn't play a role in your fears as much (though it can depending on your situation, for sure), but fearing losing the ability to *buy* food might cause a primal fear of dying to kick in.

And what's tied into losing the ability to buy food? Your careers, your bank accounts, your mortgage, your car payments, and so many other things that are tied to money. The advent of money created a wonderful exchange system to fulfill our needs, but also gave us perceptions of lack and poverty. Money is one of largest stressors in life, along with relationships.

Romantic relationships are a path to extreme enjoyment but also severe emotional pain. Any relationship, not just romantic, can be this way, especially with close family of any sort. Both money and relationships are probably the two largest sources of individual fulfillment and personal devastation on the planet. They both contribute to confidence and fear, but neither is directly responsible for each. Confidence is a place without fear, and fear is a place without confidence. It's hard for either to exist when the other is present, at least in the same context. In other words, you might fear crossing the street, but you might have confidence crossing a stream or a walkway. The point is where there's one, you typically won't find the other.

But what if you could have confidence without addressing a specific fear, like crossing the street? What if, instead, you addressed your possible fear of death? This is where things can get interesting, because if you believe that all fears are really pointing to a deeper fear inside you, where you fear death as an outcome, then what would happen to all your fears if you didn't fear death anymore? *Magic would happen*, that's what.

Remember how I walked you through the worst-case scenario in the Drill Down process? The reason I did that was to take you down a path where things got so bad that when you came back to your original fear, it didn't seem so bad after all. When you imagine just how bad things can get, what you originally feared won't have the same impact anymore. Your fears will often decrease after that point.

What if you decided to not fear death? Would that change any or all of your other fears? Using the Drill Down process on my fears, I determined that my fear of getting fired from my job really originated as a fear of death. If you're wondering how that even comes close to possible, here's my breakdown:

➡ Fear of getting fired means no money.

➡ No money means I can't pay rent.

➡ No money means I can't buy food.

➡ If I can't pay rent, I have no place to live.

➡ If I can't eat, I'll starve.

➡ If I starve, I'll die.

That's simplistic, I realize, and it doesn't include the alternatives to any of those choices. For example, I could choose to live with my parents or other family. I could borrow money or I could find more work. The list goes on, but the fear that initially kicked in when I thought of getting fired stemmed from a deep, primal fear of death. And this thought process happens at light speed, so if and when a fear comes up for you, you may not even realize that this breakdown is even happening. But once you connect the dots and figure out what means what (no job means no money means no food means…drilling down, drilling down…), you suddenly understand that it's not losing a job that you may fear. It goes deeper than that and means a lot more, which is why anxiety and stress tend to appear at times like this.

In fact, if you suffer from anxiety, this is the thought process you already know all too well. Those with anxiety often think of the worst-case scenario. This is almost exactly how anxiety is formed—by playing out this thought process to what's perceived as a dismal end. But what would happen if the end wasn't dismal? What would happen if you chose to accept that the worst-case scenario could be that you have a heart attack and die? It sounds morbid, I realize, but let's just say that you weren't afraid of that happening, would it change how you feel? Would your anxiety be different? Would it exist at all?

When my car broke down in the Arizona desert, my anxiety reached panic and I was facing my worst fear. I was scared as hell that I was going to lose my car and all my stuff because there was no way I was going to be able to get those things home, which was a thousand miles away. I almost cried, my panic was so bad.

My panic grew in intensity and kept growing until it finally reached an intolerable level. I was at my maximum and there was nowhere left to go from there. I had to accept the inevitable but I couldn't, so I "popped," so to speak. The realization that I had no other choice but to give it all up right then and there released all my fear, panic, and anxiety instantly. It was gone in milliseconds after I came to an acceptance of the worst possible outcome. The resistance I put up against losing my stuff was exactly what caused my panic in the first place. But coming to an acceptance that losing my possessions could actually be an option was what took my fears away. It was an excellent example of accepting death as an outcome. It wasn't "death" in the physical sense, but looking back at it now, I realize that losing my stuff felt like I was going to die.

THE DRILL DOWN OF THE BREAKDOWN:

➡ I am a thousand miles from home and have no money to fix my car.

➡ I'm afraid to leave my car and all my stuff because someone might take it.

➡ If someone takes it, I won't have a car and I will have lost my possessions.

➡ If I don't have a car, I can't work.

➡ If I can't work, I can't pay for housing or food.

➡ If I don't have money, my wife might leave me.

➡ If I don't have a wife, no one loves me.

➡ If I don't have a house or food, I'll die.

It's a completely different scenario with the exact same outcome: death. Of course, not feeling loved is as close to death as it can get for some people. But what would happen if you accepted not feeling loved, or even death, as a possible outcome? What would happen if you didn't fear either? Same thing as before: magic.

What you resist persists. What you fear most will be what causes you the most stress until you stop fearing it. The challenge many people run into is that they cannot turn off fear like a light switch. Much of it is ingrained or intrinsic, where it's almost hardwired and automatic. The good news is that it can be reprogrammed. For example, we're told that humans are born with two fears: The fear of loud noises and the fear of falling. But I've seen people that have gotten over both through conditioning and repeated exposure. In fact, if you ever watch parkour (free running), you'll see people jumping from rooftop to rooftop without any fear. If there are people that can override built-in fears, then you can override your learned fears.

But instead of addressing each one individually, I recommend jumping toward what you fear at the deepest level first. If you choose to believe that all fears are essentially a fear of death, imagine what life would be like if you didn't fear death! What would it be like if you accepted that both success and death were equally possible outcomes? This is what happens to many people who are very close to death. They get to a point that they can no longer stop the inevitable, so they choose to accept it as an outcome. A few years ago, I felt this very thing. I ate some bad ham and got food poisoning. I vomited more than I care to remember, and I got to a point where I literally felt like I was going to die. At that moment, I "knew" there was no turning back. I felt like death was absolutely inevitable.

You'd think, knowing death was coming, that all my fears would kick in and overcome me, but the exact opposite happened. I felt more peace and comfort than I'd ever felt in my life. In the midst of that deathly sickness, I had no more stress about anything at all. The bills I owed didn't matter anymore, my job didn't matter; in fact, everything that used to bother me completely disappeared.

I knew I was going to die, and that was alright with me. I think the reason I felt peaceful was because I realized how much stress I'd been under and how hard my relationship with my girlfriend had been. But more than that, everything I used to stress about was gone in that instant and I felt free.

But, obviously, I didn't die. In fact, when I started coming back to a healthier state, I didn't want that free feeling to end, so I tried to hang onto it. I didn't want to feel stress anymore, but sure enough, as I came back I started feeling it again. All the typical, everyday stress I felt before was back, and I was "normal" again.

Both my car breaking down in the desert and the food poisoning changed my life. I now no longer fear death. I felt like I skirted the edge of it and because of that, I feel reassured that when something similar happens, I'll be okay. Other major life events were happening around that time too, like going broke and becoming homeless. And because of that, I had many realizations, most of which consisted of understanding that even when I'm at the lowest place in my life, I'll still be fine. I may not like it, but I'll survive.

Are you afraid of dying? Do you have any fears that come up when I ask that question? If so, why? What exactly are you afraid of?

I'm not talking about suicide. That's a different thing altogether and usually plays a role for people that have a lot of unresolved, repressed emotions. If you are contemplating suicide, then reach out for help[1] before taking any final steps, because there's no turning back!

---

1   A follow-up study on those who attempted suicide by jumping off the Golden Gate Bridge found that 90 percent of the jumpers regretted their decision immediately after hitting freefall. If you are contemplating suicide, there are people who will listen to you. Please call the Suicide Prevention Lifeline in the US at 1-800-273-8255. For international numbers, visit suicide.org.

I'm talking about a fear that comes up for you when you think about dying. If you have a fear of death, why? It may sound like a silly question at first, but what exactly do you fear? For one, death is inevitable. It is the conclusion of any life and will absolutely happen to you. Choosing to fear it is like resisting an unavoidable truth. If you resist the idea of dying, you create pressure in your body and build up an immunity to happiness. Resistance creates pressure inside you. You know that's true because if you remember the last time you didn't want to accept something as true, you felt it inside of you. When you feel it in your body, that's internal conflict between what is and what you want to be. The lack of accepting what *is* creates internal struggle and will decrease your overall happiness.

I had a client once that refused to let go of her ex-boyfriend from when she was a teenager. She never wanted it to end, so she held onto the idea that someday they would be back together again. I don't have to tell you how holding on to that caused her to feel. Every relationship she had from that point on would never equal what she had when she was younger, so she stayed unhappy. Her resistance to letting that relationship go and accepting that it would never happen again kept her unhappy and lonely. But when she let go of resisting the hard truth that it would never be again, that relationship released its clutch on her life and she was able to move on and be happy.

This is how letting go of what you resist sets you free. The bigger the struggle you let go, the bigger the release. So imagine what letting go of your fear of death might feel like. You may or may not be fully conscious of why you fear death, if you do, but it plays a role in all fears that come up for you today. If, however, you chose to accept that you could die in any situation in life, do you think that fear would transform into something else?

Can Fear Die?

Try this: Think about something you fear. When you think about it, imagine that what you fear is *really* happening. You're in the reality of it and it's going on right now. You can see what's happening around you through your own eyes and hear what you'd hear as if it were real. Start to feel what you'd feel during this event.

Got it?

Now imagine in the middle of all that, *you died*, and everything that was going on suddenly disappeared. Being dead in that moment, in the midst of all your fears coming true, what happened to your fear? Knowing that what you feared is no longer there, where is your fear now?

Is it completely gone?

Realizing death could occur at any moment and is always an option incites a transformation in you and might just absolve all your fears.

IIIIIIIIIIIIIIIIIIIIIIIIIIIIIIIIIIIIIIIIIIIIIIIIIIIIIIIIIIIIIIIIIIIIIIIIIIIIIIIIIIIIIIIIIIIIIIIIIIIIIIIIIIIIIIIIIIIIIIIIIII

I realize that all this talk about death is radical and sounds so dark, but sometimes you have to think in a radically different way to feel radically different. Adopting the idea that death could happen at any time in any situation, and accepting that reality as something that just is, will free you of the chains of fear.

When I was at the height of my panic attack in the Arizona desert, realizing I was about to lose my car and everything in it, I welcomed all options to free myself of the terror I felt, and death came to my mind as an option. My panic attack made me feel like I was going to die so I asked myself, "Okay, so what if I die right now? What's wrong with that?"

I was shocked I asked myself that question! But the answer came: "I don't want to die." And I heard another part of myself respond back, "Yeah, but what if you did? What then?" And like a pressure valve, all the fear left my body. It was right at that moment I accepted death as a possible outcome to the situation I was in. It's not that I wanted to die, but accepting it as an option helped me let go of my lifelong resistance to it. And letting go of the resistance helped me release the fear. It freed me.

Accepting death as a possible outcome frees you from feeling fear. When you adopt the belief that *all* fear is a fear of death, then fear has nothing to hold on to when you accept it. It's like working at a job that you hate. You hate the hours, the people, the drive, and the pay. So once you realize you don't care about the job anymore, you no longer stress about losing it. Your work performance improves, your attitude improves, people notice you're happier, and so on. Because you let go of the fear of losing your job, you become motivated by something else instead. When fear doesn't motivate you anymore, something more positive can take its place.

I remember trying to get fired before. The more I didn't care, the more they liked me. I kept doing my job, of course, but it seemed they liked the laid-back, more authentic version of me than the fearful, "I better do what I'm told no matter what" version of me. I ended up staying a couple more years instead of quitting and actually appreciated my job again, all because I was not motivated to work by being afraid of losing my job. All because I was not motivated to work by being afraid of losing that work. Accepting that death could be what happens in a given situation, even though it rarely does happen, releases fear's hold on you.

BELIEFS DETERMINE YOUR QUALITY OF LIFE

If you do fear death and are having trouble with this concept, what are your beliefs? Some people believe that there's a divine plan for them and that their life has purpose, so even the bad stuff has meaning. If that's your belief, you may not have the fears I spoke of in this chapter. Or maybe you do because you're still working on things in yourself. Or perhaps your fear is part of the journey and it will have meaning later on in your life, like it did for me. Whatever it is, your belief will determine your quality of life. Beliefs are what you make of them so adopt ones that work for you.

I choose to believe that everything has a purpose. That way, when things go bad in my life or in the world, I will be able to handle them better and look for meaning in even the worst tragedies. For me, if the bad stuff doesn't have any meaning, I feel defeated. So I created the belief that everything has purpose and meaning so that I can process and live through the most challenging situations. It's like adopting the belief that all fear is a fear of death. I figure if I can walk tall and proud like a fearless warrior, I can handle whatever comes my way. I still have fears that come up, for sure, but I always address them and ask myself why I fear those things. I dive into what the worst-case scenario would be and experience how bad it could get. I remember that no matter how scared I am, death is actually a possibility and that if I die because of what's happening in the moment, it's okay because it will have meaning! I know I'll be fine no matter what because I've accepted that death is inevitable, both now and in the future. When you think of what you fear, let the fears play out in your head and then accept that all of it could happen, and that you could also die because of it.

I'll say it again: Radical changes require radical thinking. You know yourself better than anyone else, so do only what you can. Choosing to accept death doesn't mean you want to die, it means you are okay with whatever life throws at you and *you want to live without fears controlling you.*

Your options are unlimited, so don't weigh yourself down with fears or beliefs that no longer serve you. Anything that holds you back from making decisions that are right for you needs to be reevaluated and questioned as to whether it still serves a purpose in your life.

Everything you've read up to this point was the buildup to the final section of this chapter, which is about how to build a strong emotional foundation. When you have a strong foundation, you can walk like a warrior, with confidence and the ability to express your emotions without fear. True self-empowerment is the ability to fearlessly be yourself in the judgmental eyes of others. There's a lot of power in vulnerability, it's just a matter of building up to it, which is what we've been doing, so that you get beyond the fear of being authentically you.

HOW TO BUILD EMOTIONAL STRENGTH

I remember the day I spoke up against my bosses. In 2005, I worked for a software company. I was in a small meeting with the two co-owners of the company and they were talking down about another employee. I sat there listening as they judged my coworker's character and lack of effort. As they went on, I could feel anger bubbling up in me. The coworker wasn't there to defend himself and they were making sweeping assumptions about his work behavior. As their conversation continued, I felt compelled to say something to defend him. I knew that their perspective about the matter was very limited and even wrong in some ways, but who was I to call them out on it? After all, that would be risking my position in the company.

But the urge to say something got stronger and stronger. At the same time, I believed that speaking up would certainly be a risky venture. Besides, my rational logic was that my coworker should fight this battle on his own and that I shouldn't even be getting involved. The thought of speaking up and against what they were saying put a lot of fear into me. Did I want to get fired for standing up for a coworker? So I sat there while they talked, silently questioning my values and integrity, and wondering what someone else would do in my situation? I asked myself, "Should I risk it all in defense of someone else?

I had a major conflict going on inside myself: Do I choose to be in alignment with what I feel is right and stand up for my coworker (which might cost me my job), or should I stay quiet and let them leave the meeting believing all the stories they just told about him, which could lead him to lose his job? After I asked myself this question, the answer came.

Because I honor my values and am proud of my integrity and authenticity, I chose to speak up in spite of the fear of losing my job. I said, "With all due respect, neither of you are here to see what he does most of the time. You are making huge assumptions and pinning him under a bus when he's not even here to defend himself."

I waited for the yelling. I waited for the rage to fill their faces and for them to come at me screaming, "How dare you question our authority!" But those things never came. I waited for anything that showed how angry they were with me for butting in and making them wrong about anything. But it never happened. In fact, quite the opposite took place. One of them looked at me and said, "That's exactly what we need to hear. We aren't here most of the time, and we need that kind of input so that we know what's going on around here. Thank you for sharing that, now let's talk about this."

All of my fear disappeared. I learned in that moment that I could now and always express myself safely without them flying off the handle.

They were open to my honesty. There was no backlash for standing up for my coworker. Though really, I was standing up for myself, because it was my own integrity that I wanted to be in alignment with. I had a choice to cower and be the scared, little boy I'd always been in the past, or take a stand without fear of the consequences because I knew what was right.

> The safe path and the right path aren't always going in the same direction. But one will always keep you where you are, and the other will reinforce *who* you are.

I wanted to step out of the fear I'd held onto for so long. Right before I decided to speak up, my rationality kicked in and reminded me that I wasn't a child anymore. Also, I questioned that if I didn't stand up and choose to be vulnerable (knowing I could get yelled at or even fired), then would I be compromising who I wanted to be in life? Would I be choosing safety over honoring myself?

At the time, I had a deep-rooted value of wanting to be trusted. I knew that if I wanted people to trust me I would have to approach everything with integrity. I would have to trust and honor myself first. That meant making some hard choices, because integrity sometimes comes at the cost of comfort. But I was willing to be uncomfortable to earn that integrity. It was important to me, and I didn't want to let myself down.

One of the results of speaking up for myself and my coworker was an unexpected raise and promotion! When I originally spoke up, I felt completely exposed, as if I were a child waiting for my father to come home to discover that I just broke the living room window. Who knew that practicing authenticity would lead to admiration and respect from others? This was my first scary, yet powerful, lesson in vulnerability.

SPEAKING AUTHENTICALLY

When you show up in the world as authentic, you receive authenticity back. When you express your truths, you will get truths back. One system feeds the other and what you put into it, you get out of it. Have you ever met someone for the first time and made small talk? You talk about the weather instead of talking about what you're really thinking, like how nervous you might be, or how you have no clue what to talk about because you don't know the person.

Imagine if you said, "I have no idea what to talk about. I just met you and I don't even know if we have anything common to discuss. For all I know, I'm going to sound like an idiot when I open my mouth."

I'm sure they would be surprised to hear such honesty, but more times than not, you'll get the same type of response back: "I'm so glad you said that. I feel so awkward and I don't know what to talk about either!"

That's because your vulnerability and authenticity with them will allow them to feel the same way and open up too. It doesn't always happen that way. After all, some people choose to stay guarded no matter what. But I've learned through doing my show that the more I share of myself, my faults, my fears, and my guilt, shame, and embarrassments, the more people open up to me and feel immediately comfortable with me. They see me as real and down to earth. That's because I've chosen to be no other way but "real." I just don't have the energy to play mind games and be someone I'm not. I'd rather express my truth than put on a facade because it just takes too much energy to do so. Being yourself takes very little energy. In fact, it energizes you because you are not resisting who you are and what you want to say.

I spoke up to my bosses that day because I wanted to be in alignment with my integrity and values. Any deviation from that would have been like dishonoring myself. *Don't dishonor yourself.* Be in integrity and come from a place of truth, otherwise you'll repress what you want to express, and that leads you on a downward spiral that never seems to end. It's a path to full disconnect from your emotional self and sometimes even your physical self, because repression of emotion leads to suppression of feeling, eventually leading to depression or other not-so-pleasant states or conditions.

Each negative emotion that you choose to suppress is like adding black oil to a clear emotional pool. The more thoughts and emotions you stuff down, the more black oil fills the pool. Pretty soon, the pool is completely saturated and sludgy, and whatever was pure has completely vanished. Whatever happiness was there in the clear water is now impossible to access because there's just so much muck. The filters get clogged and everything seems to slow down and wear you out.

I realize I'm talking in metaphors, but if you think about suppressing your emotions in this way, it will give you a better idea of what's happening inside you. As that sludge builds up in you, your body and mind become more and more filled with "gunk," and happiness starts to disappear. The way to start draining that gunk is to express yourself when you are at the most vulnerable place inside of you. This is a huge leap of faith because if you're used to backing down and repressing who you are, then expressing yourself at your most vulnerable moments might seem like an impossible task. But it's *exactly* what needs to happen if you can't get out of the low space you might be in, especially if you've been in that low space for a number of years or longer.

The first time you express yourself from a place of vulnerability, you may feel fear. But it's at that very moment where you get to make a choice to be who you've always been (which will yield the same results as always) or become who you want to be (which will empower you). The focus needs to be on that moment, not what will happen in the aftermath. Focusing on the moment and who you want to be keeps you in the perfect space to make decisions that are right for you. If, instead, you shift your focus and start thinking a few minutes ahead, you will start to come up with stories of what might happen, causing you to deviate from making an empowering decision. You will get stuck where you've always gotten stuck in the past. The most empowering decision is made when you base it on what's happening now, not what might happen afterward when you've had time to consider the consequences.

Showing up in the world as genuinely confident involves allowing yourself to be vulnerable and share a part of you that you might feel uncomfortable sharing. The first time you share is the hardest, but the second time, knowing that you survived the first time, is easier. From that point on, your confidence, self-esteem, self-worth, and emotional strength grows and grows. And soon, you'll have no problem speaking your truth, even when there's a chance of loss.

Whether you're with family, friends, coworkers, your boss, your partner, or whoever, when you are in alignment with your truth and decide to express that truth (knowing full well that the person you're expressing it to might not like it, and may even want you out of their life), you will develop a mental resilience and feeling of assuredness you've never felt before.

Expressing yourself in vulnerable moments can get you one of two results:

1. Those who love and support you will love and support you even more because they see that you are honoring yourself. They want you to be happy and healthy, and the more authentic you are with them, the closer they'll be able to get to you. If, however, you wear the body armor of inauthenticity or invulnerability, it will be hard for others to connect with you at a deeper level. When you take that armor off and show that you trust them with your innermost thoughts and feelings, you create a bond like you've never felt before.

2. People won't know how to behave around you now that you are changing. They may not even want you in their life anymore because they feel uncomfortable that you are honoring yourself. This is harder to accept because the goal isn't necessarily to drive people away from you, it's to become the most empowered you possible. But then again, if people are uncomfortable with your honoring yourself, maybe it's best that they're not in your life.

If someone doesn't like who you've become, it's because they don't want you to change or evolve. They want you to stay the same so that they themselves don't have to change. They may have an unhealthy dependency on you staying who you are to keep them in a dysfunctional place. This isn't always the case, as sometimes people grow to like the persona that you've been showing them over the years. So they may see this new, authentic you and realize they prefer the mask you wore previously.

But as you know, wearing a mask all the time just makes you tired. You can't be fake forever. Eventually you grow very tired of showing the world someone you're not. That's why it's so important to embrace your faults, your shame, your guilt, and everything else that doesn't feel so good and let it be a part of you. It's like telling the world, "Hey, I have a lot of strengths but I also have weaknesses, and I'm okay with both because I'm not perfect."

Expressing yourself in your most vulnerable moments is a process of baby steps, but when you do, it builds a happier, healthier you. It doesn't mean you tell *everyone everything* about yourself all the time, it just means you take small steps and share with people you feel safe with first. Usually, that's intimate partners or friends and family. But some people feel safer with complete strangers, so they may befriend someone and just pour their heart out. The idea is to convey emotions that are stuck in you so that they can be released. When you do this, you allow the emotional energy to flow in your body. You feel lighter, more energized and more passionate. Want to try that right now?

Think of someone you know that you would feel safe with and imagine that they are standing (or sitting) right in front of you. If you can't think of anyone, make someone up! Who would be the safest person in the world that you could share anything with and not be judged by or made to feel bad or wrong?

You might imagine a relative or friend, or maybe a character you've seen in a movie. How about someone spiritual or in religious texts? Once you have someone in mind, share with them your deepest secrets. Share your shame, guilt, embarrassments, fears and anything else that comes to mind. Know that they won't judge you or think you're broken or bad. Don't exaggerate or sugarcoat anything. Take an opportunity to be the most vulnerable you've ever been.

|||||||||||||||||||||||||||||||||||||||||||||||||||||||||||||||||||||||||||||||||||||||||||||||||||||||||||||||||||||||||

To express what you feel in the moment is the ultimate pressure release system, but it is a challenging road to take because it involves a leap of faith. Sometimes you don't feel safe around certain people so you back off and hold off, so as to not expose your vulnerabilities. However, the more you're able to express yourself while being vulnerable, the more bricks go into that strong emotional foundation you're trying to create.

All it takes is a few baby steps to say what's on your mind. The first giant leap through fear is the stepping stone to the second, smaller jump—knowing you survived the first giant leap. Don't focus on the outcome, focus on what you need to do in the moment. As you repeat this process more and more, you'll find out just how easy it is to express who you are in the world authentically and even willingly. If you can't find anyone to do it with, just do the exercise above in your mind so that you have some outlet in which to express. Over time, you'll experience the most freeing feeling there is. It's a release from your own emotional prison.

CHAPTER 8
Maintaining Forward Momentum

There are probably hundreds, if not more, processes, resources, and exercises beyond this book that you could add to your personal growth tool box. You could go to therapy, get coaching, read more books, watch self-help videos, or listen to personal development podcasts all day long, but still not absorb everything simply because that type of learning is not *experiential*. In other words, you can read books and take classes on learning how to fly a plane, but until you're in the cockpit, you'll never understand the entire process as well as you could. Learning the steps, then doing the steps need to go hand in hand so that you develop an unconscious competence in your ability to handle all the challenges that will absolutely come your way.

Your behavior and reactions to challenges will determine your level of long-term satisfaction and happiness in life. If you respond to the challenges "functionally," where you honor what's right for you and make decisions that empower you, you will feel more at peace more of the time. If you respond to the challenges in life "dysfunctionally," you create an unhealthy forward momentum of stress and misery.

In the moment of a challenge, there may be a tendency to take the easy path—the one you believe creates the least conflict. However, in the long term, this path can create underlying unhappiness and you can walk around feeling like there's got to be more to life than what you're living. If, however, you choose the path that's "right," where you are in alignment with your values and beliefs and make a decision that is the most empowering to you, you might feel the immediate stress or pain of the moment, but that feeling will be short-lived. Sometimes the right choice is the hardest one to make, but the one that is best for all involved.

Sometimes your choice will hurt other people's feelings, but in the end, it's the one that allows for the most growth and healing for everyone involved. Staying in dysfunction exacerbates dysfunction, so make the right choice for you whenever you can. It's not always easy, and sometimes it's not even possible, but you do the best you can. And you may need to take a few baby steps just to get an idea that you can do it. They will seem like massive leaps over a chasm, but after you make it over the first time, the jumps feel shorter and shorter. In order to help you take those leaps, I've created a Self-Empowerment Checklist that you can refer to whenever you're in a challenging situation, so that you are always moving toward keeping and strengthening your power.

The most important concept for you to take from this book is the idea of keeping or giving away your power. Self-empowerment is a lifelong pursuit and maintenance plan. It gets easier and easier with every difficult situation you overcome. It's not because the challenges get easier, it's that you become wiser and get to know just the type of behavior that takes away your power. When you keep your power, *everyone* wins. Use the checklist on the following pages as both a reminder of how to keep your power and a reference for making decisions that are right for you.

THE SELF-EMPOWERMENT CHECKLIST

Use this checklist of empowering declarations and reminders whenever you face a decision, run into a challenge, or need reassurance that you're going in the right direction. Think of these as a philosophical view of an empowering life, not as absolutes that work in every situation.

- ❏ I am in alignment with what's most important to me (my values).
- ❏ I am not being influenced by my fear of the consequences.
- ❏ I am taking steps toward honoring myself.
- ❏ I am making decisions based on what I really want for myself.
- ❏ My decisions are meant to empower others, not control them.
- ❏ Those that have the most influence in my life support my honoring myself.
- ❏ I do not change because of what others want, I change because of what I want.
- ❏ I honor people where they are, not where I want them to be.
- ❏ I make decisions based on who I am and want to be, not who I *was*.
- ❏ I am not enabling other people's dysfunctions.
- ❏ I am fulfilling my needs first so I have enough to give to others, if I so choose.
- ❏ When someone triggers me, I focus on healing myself, not changing them.
- ❏ I question fears that I've held onto since childhood.

- [ ] My fear, anger, or upset in the moment could be an old emotional trigger and may not have the same meaning as it once did.

- [ ] What I want is just as important as what other people want.

- [ ] I am being compassionate to myself first, *then* to others.

- [ ] I don't have to wear my emotional armor all the time.

- [ ] People can hurt me only if I let them take my power.

- [ ] I am not judging others to avoid what I need to heal in myself.

- [ ] I am a contributor to my own happiness and unhappiness because of the paths I choose and the people I choose to be with.

- [ ] The people I choose to be close to are a direct reflection of my level of healing and growth.

- [ ] I understand that I can create unhealthy relationships by seeking in others what's missing in me.

- [ ] I am working on healing my fears so that those fears don't manifest in my relationships.

- [ ] It is not someone else's job to make me happy.

- [ ] Pleasing others is okay; pleasing others to the point where I feel resentful is not.

- [ ] I take time to myself to be with my own thoughts.

- [ ] What's true for me isn't always true for others, but that doesn't make me wrong.

- [ ] My emotional strength builds when I express my shame, fear, doubt, guilt, and pain with someone safe.

- [ ] If it doesn't feel right, it isn't.

- ❑ Honoring my boundaries lets others know what's acceptable to me and what's not.

- ❑ I keep toxic people at a distance.

- ❑ I am allowed to feel angry.

- ❑ People will have no choice but to accept that I have made my share of mistakes and am going to make more.

- ❑ I acknowledge the mistakes I make.

- ❑ I say No when I mean No, and Yes when I mean Yes.

- ❑ I am choosing to be me instead of the person others want me to be.

- ❑ I am not responsible for others' reactions or feelings.

- ❑ I forgive myself.

In 2005, I experienced an emotional breakdown. I was depressed, still recovering from a breakup, and in a very new relationship that was about to end. The perfect storm of emotions finally got the best of me and I fell to my knees and cried. My girlfriend witnessed this breakdown and comforted me the best she could, allowing me to express things I had never said out loud. I wasn't aware that I had held onto so many years of hatred and anger about my stepfather.

The day after that event was very strange for me. I felt like I had released 35 years of anger and had never viewed the world without it. I never considered myself an angry person before that, but how could I have? I had always repressed it, never letting it come to the surface. So it came out in other ways. Some people in my life called my behavior passive aggressive. I called it "something wrong with me." Either way, it was my *normal.*

But that version of normal was what held me back from enjoying the full depth of what life had to offer. It was strange to wake up the morning after my breakdown with no anger or hatred in me because I had never experienced that before. My identity was wrapped up in everything I'd held onto since I was a child, so I didn't understand the world any other way. Reality without repressed anger was like being born into a world I didn't recognize.

If you've not been able to get past some of the blocks in your life, you may have such a firm grasp on everything you've been that you don't want to let it go because…who are you without it? That can be the scariest yet most exciting part of the journey. It's scary to think you are letting go of a part of yourself that you've gotten to know so well—a part you feel very comfortable with (even though it probably made you *un*comfortable). But letting it go will free you to have thoughts you've never had before, the kind of thoughts that aren't tainted by the filters that have altered your perceptions most of your life. Once the filters are gone, you may not know who you are anymore. But that's a good thing!

You may need to feel the loss of who you were to make room for who you want to be. This new you will have different beliefs and values and see the world as an entirely different place. *Keeping* this new version of you is heavily dependent on the choices you make from that point on. If you choose to stay in toxic environments with toxic people, or you're too afraid to express your truths, or you spend more time being overly compassionate to others but showing little to no compassion for yourself, you know where you'll end up—right where you don't want to be. That may even be where you are right *now*, so if you don't necessarily like everything about where you are in life, it's vital that you start putting more time and energy into your healing and growth. That way you can start making the right decisions for you.

You will probably experience some losses along the way, I won't lie. When you heal and grow, there are those that won't want you to change. They are comfortable with who you are so they may try to convince you in many ways to stay the same.

Make sure to keep evolving emotionally and to not be tempted (or coerced) by others that might want to take you off the path of growth and healing. And as you learn new things about yourself, there will be even more experiences to challenge those learnings. Remember that you will have all the tools you need to get through those challenges. The test is whether or not you choose to use those tools. Honoring your boundaries is a great example of that. It's easy to read about, and perhaps a little less easy to implement with strangers, but doing it with people that have known you for a long time? That's when the true test of what you know takes place and you are presented with the choice of keeping your power or giving it away.

You don't have to pass every test in life, so it will be okay to skip some of them. But don't skip too many, or you may lose the opportunity to apply what you've learned. As soon as you apply your learnings once, it sets the precedent for what you'll do for similar challenges in the future. It *will* get easier over time, but you have to do it at least once to get the ball rolling. After that, you'll build your emotional core until you are strong enough to handle almost anything that comes your way.

You've got this. You can take the reins of your life back. It isn't something anyone else can do for you, so you have to do it yourself. You will absolutely run into limitations that will seem impossible to overcome, *but you can overcome them.* You couldn't possibly have survived up to this point in life without something way inside you motivating you to keep going. Whenever you do any personal growth work, that's proof that there is something greater inside of you wanting to break through and create a better life for you.

I want you to achieve full empowerment so that you are able to express your true self without fear. It is a place where you stand tall instead of feeling small. There's not enough time on this planet to live in fear or be submissive to others. So why come here to live in misery and overwhelm that incredible brain of yours when all you have to do is make a choice, take a leap of faith, and be the person you want to express instead of the one who chooses to repress?

Life is about the full range of the human experience: all the pain, the joy, the peace and the chaos, all wrapped into a body and mind that is absolutely capable of handling it. You choose how you show up in each and every moment. You won't always know right away how to handle every challenge that presents itself, but you'll always have a choice on how to respond. And the choice you make will either empower you or take that power away, so do your best to make the most empowering choices so that you can live the most powerful life possible.

You can do this. *You are amazing.*

Index

A

Abuse: emotional, 48; physical, 47–49, 53–54

"Abused mind" concept, 111–12

Abusive relationships, 46–50, 83–84, 91

Accepting problems, as choice, 58, 85–86, 92–95

Adapting to problems, as choice, 80–82

Addictive behavior, 129

Anxiety, 132–33, 146–47

Assertiveness, in decision-making, 42–45

Attraction, 122–24

Authenticity, in relationships, 29, 33, 109–12, 124–30, 157–61

B

Beliefs, limiting, 74–76

Boundaries: personal, 29, 30–32, 38; in relationships, 111–12

C

Choices: in boundaries, 30–32; in relationships, 76–86, 92–95, 120–21

Codependency, 87; problems, 114

Cohen, Alan, quoted, 4

Commitments, 5–11

Compassion, 36–40

Compulsive fear response, 136–38

Congruence, 4, 9–10

Consequences, and fear, 143

D

Death, and fear, 144–52

Decision-making, 40–45, 62–69; exercise, 66–67

Defeat, as liberating factor, 81

Desperation, 97

Dissociation, 49, 53

Drill Down process: and death, 144–52; exercise, 142; and fears, 133–43; secondary process, 141–43

Dysfunction: in relationships, 112–15; and healing, 101–103; prolonging, 118–22

Dysfunctional Feedback Machine, 101–103

E

Emotional abuse, 48

Emotional foundation, building, 154–56

Emotional Freedom Technique (EFT), 50–53, 78–79

Acknowledgments

Over the last several years I've written over one million words for my blog and other websites, so I thought writing a book would be a piece of cake. I couldn't have been more wrong. It was hard and it took a lot of time.

There's no way I could have accomplished this on my own, so I'd like to thank the following people for their amazing contributions toward the creation of this book and for keeping me sane:

Renee, Bridget, and the entire team at Ulysses Press who put their faith in me to accomplish what at times seemed like an impossible task. Without them, this book would not have seen the light of day.

My girlfriend, Asha Lightbearer, who has taught me so much about love, connection, and what a healthy, functional relationship is supposed to be. I love you!

My incredible mom, who managed to survive a 40+ year abusive relationship and welcome me back into her home after my divorce. Everything my mom has done for me could fill a book. I am so proud of you, thank you for everything.

The dedicated Facebook group for the book launch. You guys and girls were so valuable, and your input helped make this book what it has become. I am honored you invested your time and energy into me.

The brilliant and awesome listeners and supporters of The Overwhelmed Brain podcast. You've shared your struggles with me, you've reached out and thanked me, and you've listened time and time again even when I thought no one was listening. Without you, there would be no show, and certainly no book! Thank you.

The impeccable TOB Patron Program members. You are huge—thank you so much!

Those who gave me the strength and determination to run with the ball and never quit: Dean, Amber, Mo, Aaron, Owen, Anthony, Austin, Michael, Justin, Alex, Celest, Navid, Lauri, Jade, John, Kate, and so many more.

Greg, for caring and sharing; Abdelmoumene, for being a super nice guy; Federico, for taking massive steps; Tim, for really getting it; Scott, for your authentic self; Billy, for keeping it real; Lena, for pushing through some huge barriers; Jamie, Lori, Lizzy, Debbie, and so many more that have made an impact in my life—I'm grateful for you.

Finally, my family. My mom, late dad, and sisters and brothers are all phenomenal people that I'm proud to be related to. They have shown me unparalleled, unconditional love that I can't even begin to reciprocate. Thank you all.

Thank you for investing your time into this book. And to the reader: Thank you for investing your time into this book. I appreciate you.

About the Author

Paul Colaianni is a personal empowerment coach, author, and host of the top-rated, award-winning personal growth podcast called The Overwhelmed Brain. His passion is to empower people so that they can make decisions that are right for them. Life-changing episodes and articles can be found on his website at theoverwhelmedbrain.com